T5-AVP-902

CONCILIUM

concilium 1992/1

TOWARDS THE AFRICAN SYNOD

Edited by

G. Alberigo and
A. Ngindu Mushete

SCM Press Ltd
London

Copyright © 1991 Stichting Concilium
English translations © 1991 SCM Press Ltd

All rights reserved. No part of this publication may be reproduced, stored in a retrieval system, or transmitted, in any form or by any means, electronic, mechanical, photocopying, recording or otherwise, without the prior written permission of Stichting Concilium, Prins Bernhardstraat 2, 6521 AB Nijmegen, The Netherlands.

February 1992

ISBN: 0334 03012–9

Typeset at The Spartan Press Ltd, Lymington, Hants
Printed by Mackays of Chatham, Kent

Concilium: Published February, April, June, August, October, December.

BX
880
.C7
1992
vol.1

LIBRARY
JESUIT SCHOOL OF THEOLOGY
1100 EAST 55th STREET
CHICAGO, ILLINOIS 60615

Contents

The Future of *Concilium*

About this time last year I was giving an account of the Concilium Congress at Louvain. I recalled the various phases through which the journal had passed: the dissemination and development of the achievements of the Second Vatican Council, followed by openness to the humanities and to interdisciplinary studies, and then the priority accorded to new figures like women and Third World theologians. And I remarked that the Louvain Congress was the fruit of all these developments. It stressed their importance, but it did not indicate any clear line for the future. I felt that new guidelines were absolutely necessary where friendship, a shared intellectual climate and the rejection of certain current retrograde positions were not enough to define the identity of a publication. At the annual business meeting in Wiesbaden last Pentecost, many contributions were made in this direction, and while we are waiting for the result of certain organizational consequences which are in preparation, it seems legitimate to single out some markers which already seem quite firmly established.

A first question could occur to those who took part in the Louvain Congress, even more than to those who were at the Brussels Congress twenty years earlier – where fewer divergent voices could be heard but where the different trends in theology were better represented. Is *Concilium* still a journal, or has it become a movement in the church? That question can be answered quite clearly. Without doubt there is a trend within the church which recognizes itself in *Concilium*. However, that trend is not led, far less organized, by us, and we are in no way its unique organ of expression. Our sole responsibility when we meet is for the journal. And it is the interests of the journal that we must be concerned to define carefully.

Contradictory concerns are expressed in the columns of *Concilium*, in the answers to questionnaires sent out by some of the publishers, and in the reactions heard during the Congress, not to mention among the editorial directors. It is said that the journal should become more 'scientific' again, but also that it should be more readable for a wider public; the 'sections' are very important in preserving its 'academic' character, but priority must be given to the 'themes' and from now on production must be organized around them; the international character which is a distinctive feature of the journal must be maintained, but here justice must be done to the current regionalization of theology, otherwise the result will be an abstract and ultimately uninteresting universality. More profoundly, a twofold appeal for increased attention to both culture and the religions – which today are in confrontation – and for a greater pastoral sensitivity stands over against the desire to see the journal maintain the strictly theological character which has defined it so far.

In this connection one decision emerged quite clearly from our discussions: *Concilium* must preserve its 'theological' character. By that is meant a reflection carried out in faith, which at the same time becomes increasingly open to cultural life and to other religions, and involvement in ecclesial praxis. The journal must also remain 'theological' in the sense of maintaining real intellectual rigour, even if the words 'scientific' or 'academic' are neither very adequate nor very realistic. The problem of readability is another matter, and (in some editions) that perhaps relates above all to the translations. As for the relationship between the sections and the themes, though the former remain to guarantee this intellectual rigour, it has been agreed that in practice the latter have priority and are subsequently attached to the sections to which they are akin. That is what we have been doing for several years, in full awareness of the compromise that we are making.

If *Concilium* defines itself as being theological, should it also remain formally 'Catholic', or has the time come to give it an ecumenical character? That is another question which is often asked. It is by no means easy to resolve. Why? Because the very people who say that 'confessional' adherence is out of date are often those who call for vigorous ecclesial involvement in the Catholic communion. Now these two requests are contradictory, and the degree of weight carried by *Concilium* in this church presupposes the affirmation of an identity. All the same, there is no question here either of a 'confessional' spirit or of complete structural rigidity: *Concilium* also seeks to express the openness inherent in the term 'Catholic'. Not only must the journal involve theologians from other churches more in its publication, in editorial committees and at least symbolically among its editorial directors, but we also want increasingly to allow members of other religions, of other intellectual and spiritual families, to have their say. Just as the words 'catholic' or 'ecumenical' can have broader or narrower connotations, so can the term 'conciliar', at which our name hints. If the church is 'people of God', in the sense that the community has priority over the institution, *the* people of God in a deeper sense is the whole of humanity, and one can speak of a 'conciliar process' which involves a coming together to meet the great challenges faced by human beings at this time.

The name of the journal also raises in an acute way, twenty-five years after its foundation, the problem of its relationship to Vatican II. It was born under this sign: does that sign still determine its identity? At Wiesbaden it became clear that there was a unanimous conviction on this point. Though we may sometimes have neglected to refer to the Council in our pages, we nevertheless keep returning to it as an essential heritage. And we are persuaded that this decision does not restrict us, but calls us to a vigorous dynamism. Nor do we think of this reference to the Council as a work of exegesis, indispensable in its place but a very feeble way of doing theology, and for fifteen years outmoded as an approach to the problems we now face. We understand our link with the Council primarily as creative fidelity, starting from these very texts, to the intentions – and (one also might say) to the major intuitions or the spirit – of John XXIII and the Council. Certainly there is no disguising some of the ambiguities in the way in which the Council has been developed. One might think of the tensions between the ecclesiology of the people of God and the hierarchology of Vatican I, between the apostolate of the laity and clerical structures, between the world seen as a subject of the divine plan and the church which alone discerns the signs of this plan, between pragmatic religious liberty and a foundation which is strictly based on the gospel, between the recognition of the religions and ecclesiocentrism, etc. But is the New Testament itself, taken as a whole, any less prodigal? Is not doing theology always a matter of interpretation by choosing one's preferred perspectives?

We feel on more solid ground when we relate our fidelity – secondarily – above all to the *event* of the Council, so prodigious, so unexpected in the development of the church, even for contemporaries who were outside it. It was an open spiritual event, and since then it has run its course, despite all opposition. It was an event which inaugurated a permanent self-reformation. It was the event of a church which took the risk of wanting to 'see its reflection in the gospel'. It was an event which showed at the same time, paradoxically, both a desire to become more human for the sake of the faith, and a freedom affirmed in the face of what was 'too human', the various forms of compromise with society, the egoism, injustice and materialism which the 'Christian' past does not disguise very well. Can the priority of concern for the poorest, for the struggle for peace, for the safeguarding of creation, serve as a touchstone for such a fidelity without constituting a new 'canon in the canon' or justifying a kind of racism in reverse?

The interpretation of the message and even more of the event of the Council brings us back to a present reality which still motivates our concern to locate ourselves clearly in relation to it. At present its 'reception' is taking place from different perspectives, and we are constantly confronted with a series of rereadings: material (as a form of reference), reductionist (in terms of reducing effective or potential openings) and deductive (when it is thought possible once and for all to get away from morality, structures, law, rites abstractly deduced from 'doctrine'). We are familiar with this process, and we know how councils can be 'received' in a variety of ways: acceptance or rejection, amplification or minimalization, openness or a closedness which can amount to diversion. We also know how it is possible to forget the diversities which have led to the framing of the texts and are an essential condition for understanding them, with the result that priority is given to a pedantic approach based on the letter of the texts. The apparatus of the church is familiar with these procedures, as is evident from the history of the Council of Chalcedon and even more that of the Council of Trent. Nor are they just theoretical; they are also practical, and relate to the choice of ways of implementing conciliar guidelines or decisions, and appointing the people to be entrusted with this task. As far as Vatican II is concerned, it is enough to mention as edifying examples the series of episcopal conferences and synods, the discussions on the relationship between the Council and the church crisis of the 1970s, the weight accorded to traditionalism, the credit given or refused to theological research, and the attitude to bilateral ecumenical commissions and to eucharistic communion between the churches. The reference to the Council also evokes a real struggle in the church.

So, in conclusion, it is important to be clear in what sense we can speak at *Concilium* of a 'struggle' in this sphere. Our own attitude is essentially innovative. We are concerned to propose or to support new creative initiatives, as means of expression for the confession of faith, liturgy, ethics, church institutions. We are concerned to justify, on the basis of Christian freedom, an alienable right to test them, even if this means running counter to disciplines and directives emanating from the authorities. And we are concerned to do that without intolerant and sterile (and in some cases malicious) polemic against other positions and other interpretations, even if, because they are official, they have a power which they are abusing. 'The fruit of the Spirit is love, joy, peace, patience, kindness, goodness, faithfulness, gentleness, self-control; against such there is no law.'

It is essential for *Concilium* to have a future. And there is no place for doubting this, despite the difficulties. On the contrary, we are full of hope. But in keeping with the gospel, this future comes at the cost of the risk of this freedom and this respect for others.

Jean-Pierre Jossua

Translated by John Bowden

Editorial

Almost three years ago, *Concilium* readily agreed to devote a special issue to the Synod for Africa which was announced by John Paul II at the beginning of 1989. In this way it emphasized the extraordinary importance of this assembly not only for the churches of Africa but also for Christians of the other continents.

The preparation of the issue has been inspired by a wish to make available to our African brothers and sisters some means – modest though they may be – of reflection, discussion and also communication.

Unfortunately this editorial has had to be written in the name of a European, not by way of prevarication, but as a result of the difficulties which have dogged the whole issue. The difficulty of attribution is the last but by no means the only one. Of course there have been difficulties over communication, a problem over which most of Africa still suffers. However, there have been even greater difficulties as a result of the marginalization of what is left of the preparation of the Synod. Only a few isolated Africans have grasped its importance, and the Roman officials have exploited this lack of concern, drawing all the acts of preparation into the centre. As a result it has proved very difficult to call attention to the Synod and to involve bishops, theologians and Christian groups in preparations for it. At most any success has been spasmodic. (It proved impossible to get an article from Penoukou to illustrate the requests being made within the African churches in connection with the Synod.)

Is this another wasted opportunity?

The present issue has been planned, with the full agreement of my colleague Ngindu Mishete, and with the benefit of advice from a number of African bishops and theologians, in such a way as to provide a panorama of the major problems arising in Africa in connection with the plan for the Synod. A first group of contributions seeks to focus on the rich, if distant, heritage of the African synodical tradition (Dujarier) and the main features of the local churches (Uzukwu) which are approaching the third millennium in Africa in very different situations and with very different problems (Silota and Maimela: it was impossible to secure an article from Mgr Tshibangu). Special attention has been paid to ecclesial experiences in an Islamic context, which perhaps antici-pate a situation which could also become common for other churches in the southern hemisphere (Teissier, Onaiyekan).

These articles should have been followed by a contribution on the relationship between the Synod and the reception of Vatican II in Africa: this was a very important link, but unfortunately the difficulties confront-ing Mgr Zoa, who had undertaken to write it, proved too great.

The political and social scene in which the preparation for the Synod is taking place is of great importance, all the more so in the present phase of rapid and radical changes all over the planet. Despite the extreme fluidity of this scene, it was felt appropriate to include a rapid analysis (Riccardi), regardless of the risk that at least in some respects it might prove to be out of date by the time the issue was published.

Again, the analysis of the *Lineamenta* would have been longer and more varied had the articles asked for from Bimwenyi Kweshi and Ela arrived; all that is left is the contribution by Ukpong.

It was clearly vital to stress how important it was for attention to be paid to the Synod by other Catholic churches (Luneau) and by non-Roman Catholic African Christians (Zoé-Obianga, Parthenios); we also attempted, vainly, to obtain a Muslim view on the Synod.

A last section contains information of considerable interest. First come some very perceptive reflections from Mgr Agre on the work of the preparatory commission. Then there is an analysis of the current view of Christianity in Africa in European public opinion (de Gendt). There follows a survey of the long road from the project for an African council to the convening of the Synod (Mveng), and finally an interesting but necessarily problematical approach to the crucial theme of 'inculturation' (Metena M'nteba).

The issue ends with reflections (Alberigo) on the importance that the African Synod cannot fail to have. Either it will prove a stage in the growth of Christian awareness, or African Catholicism will remain a prisoner of pessimism, indifference and the tentacles of bureaucracy.[1]

Giuseppe Alberigo

Notes

1. We still have no information about forms of participation in the Synod or what course it will follow. 29 June 1991 saw the publication of the Roman decisions for the analogous conference of the Latin American episcopate, to be held in Santo Domingo in October 1992. There are provisions for the episcopal conferences to elect their own representatives in the proportion of one to five (but the Brazilian conference is

penalized because above one hundred members the proportion becomes one in ten). The pope, for his part, will convene an indefinite number of other Latin American bishops. The Holy See will publish appropriate procedural rules for the conference, but none are yet known, nor will any be framed in collaboration with the Latin American episcopate. It is easy to see that if similar criteria are used for the African Synod, the pessimism and lack of interest will be further extended.

I · The African Synodical Tradition

Michel Dujarier

To speak of the 'synodical tradition' is to enter a field of study as vast as the church. The church is, in fact, *koinonia*, communion, so all its activities are necessarily marked by a certain synodical character. The use of the term 'synodia' by the first Christians is an illuminating sign of this. The word, which originally means 'journey together', is also sometimes used to denote the liturgical assembly, and above all the church itself. So Irenaeus speaks of the '*synodia* of the brethren', Julius Africanus salutes the '*synodia* in the Spirit' and the Liturgy of St James prays for the '*synodia* of the orthodox', the '*synodia* in Christ'.

What about the term *synodos*? Over and above its primitive sense of 'travelling companion', it too denotes the liturgical assembly, but its usual meaning among Christians is a meeting of a conciliar kind. We may recall here that at the church's beginnings, synod and council were completely synonymous, *concilium* being the Latin equivalent of the Greek *synodos*. From Nicaea onwards the Latins, who in the third century spoke only of *concilium*, also gradually came to use the term *synodos* in the same sense.[1]

In speaking of the 'African' synodical tradition I shall limit the field of research to two regions on the present-day continent of Africa which have played an important part in the life of the church, Egypt and North Africa, with their two respective capitals, Alexandria and Carthage. We shall look at the synodical practice of these communities only on their own territory, since the part that they played in councils abroad would take us too far afield. We shall see that they regularly held local, provincial or even regional councils, showing a real desire to share concerns with their sister churches. We shall study them over three periods in which this approach was particularly characteristic. First we shall look at the church of Carthage in the middle of the third century, stamped by the personality and action of Cyprian, and then at the church of Alexandria, where Athanasius was particularly prominent in the Arian period. Finally we shall return to North Africa to examine the synods in the long Donatist dispute, which was followed by the problem of Pelagianism. Here Aurelius, primate of Carthage, and Augustine of Hippo are the main figures.

I The church of Carthage: Cyprian

The first African synod which has left traces in history is the one held at Carthage under Agrippinus, surrounded by seventy bishops, around 220. Confronted with the problem of the return of converted heretics, the synod sanctioned (re)baptism as the usage of the African church. Between 236 and 240 a new regional synod was held at the same place, this time with about ninety bishops, under the presidency of Donatus. Faced with the 'numerous and grave offences' committed by Privatus of Lambaesis, primate of Numidia, the assembly felt obliged to depose him from office.[2]

It was above all during the ten years of the episcopate of Cyprian (249–58) that the synodical tradition of North Africa began to manifest itself. Two major problems then arose: what attitude was to be taken to repentant apostates, and how was it possible to justify the African practice of the (re)baptism of heretics, when the Roman Christians had the opposite custom? Four councils met at Carthage between 251 and 254 to answer the first question. The second was considered by three others, held in 255 and 256. Without going into detail over the decisions taken,[3] let us try to discover what spirit prevailed at these assemblies.

What is significant is the concern expressed by Cyprian always to work together as a church. 'To the priests and deacons, his brothers,' he writes that his desire is 'to study in common what is required by the government of the church and, having examined it together, to decide on just what is to be done.' In connection with a problem which some priests have put to him, he adds: 'I have not been able to reply to this all by myself, for since the beginning of my episcopate I have made it a rule not to decide anything on the basis of my own personal opinion without your advice and the approval of the people' (*Ep*. 14.1, 2, 4). Certainly the bishop is in the last instance the one who decides, but he does not do so without first having taken the advice of his clergy and obtained the agreement of his community. 'It befits modesty and discipline, and the very life that we should all lead, for the leaders assembled with the clergy, in the presence of those of the people who have not fallen, to order all things after scrupulous examination in common deliberation' (*Ep*. 19.2, 2). To the clergy of Rome who consult him by letter Cyprian similarly affirms: 'I do not think that I should give my opinion in isolation. I must know details of these cases and study the solution carefully, not only with my colleagues, but with all the people. It is important to think about everything and weigh it carefully before making a ruling which will constitute a precedent for the future' (*Ep.* 34.4.1).

This concern for shared reflection, which here involves the church of a particular place, recurs in an identical way in the case of a regional council. The preamble to the 'Sentences of the Eighty-Seven Bishops' of Africa, Numidia and Mauritania who gathered in a synod at Carthage on 1 September 256 brings this out nicely.[4] These 'fellow bishops', who describe themselves as 'well beloved colleagues', and 'brothers', have 'met as one body (*in unum convenire*)', representing their various provinces. They are there 'with priests and deacons, and also in the presence of the greater part of the people'. After summing up their joint view on the need 'to baptize with the baptism of the church and to sanctify the heretics who come to the church', Cyprian says: 'It is important for each of us to say what he thinks about these matters, without judging anyone and without refusing the right of self-expression to anyone who thinks otherwise.' The principle is to allow each participant to give his personal opinion quite freely: 'In fact, none should set himself up as a bishop of bishops or constrain his colleagues to acquiesce by a tyrannical terror, since every bishop has his own judgment which is guaranteed by his freedom and his power; and he cannot be judged by another bishop any more than he himself can judge another bishop.' So the Primate of Carthage asks each of his eighty-six fellow bishops to give their opinions and to sign. The conciliar meeting is not in fact an ordinary assembly; it is an *in unum convenire*, which aims at arriving at a unanimous decision.

However, this consensus has a special character, because it is based on scripture and the witness of tradition. As Sieben quite rightly remarks,[5] as well as a horizontal dimension – the unanimity of the bishops from all the provinces – the consensus has a vertical dimension by virtue of this reference to revelation and the life of the church. The bishops have reflected and decided 'in conformity to the demands of faith, charity and the concerns of the time'. Moreover, this consensus is connected with the action of the Holy Spirit; it is an event which is the work of God himself (*Ep.* 57.5. 1–2).

I should add that the 'synodical letters' sent after each assembly to all the bishops of the region and even beyond, far from simply passing on information, are a call to join in the consensus established at the time of the council. These letters can meet with the agreement of the church of Rome, as in the case of the decision taken on the question of the penance to be given to repentant apostates. But the church of Rome can also prove to hold the opposite view, as in the case of Pope Stephen on the baptism of heretics; the question then has to be taken up again and a mature decision arrived at in further and more comprehensive gatherings, until the day when unanimity prevails.

II The Alexandrian councils: Athanasius

We have good documentation for the synodical practice of North Africa in the middle of the third century, but much less for the church of Egypt in the same period. Only two sets of facts are reported, unfortunately not very precisely.

Two synods were held in Alexandria by Demetrius in 231 and 232 in connection with the expulsion of Origen.[6] The first brought together a number of Egyptian bishops and some priests: they banned the famous head of the theological school from teaching and banished him from the city. The second, composed only of a small number of bishops, and without priests, reduced him to lay status. A synodical letter was sent to all the churches, but those of Palestine, Arabia, Phoenicia and Achaea did not accept the decisions of the synod because of their esteem for Origen. Eusebius of Caesarea also tells us that around 252, Dionysius of Alexandria arrived in the province of Fayyum, where he convened an important meeting in the nome of Arsinoe to put to rights the beliefs of the sectarian followers of Nepos, the old bishop of the place, who had written a work with a millenarian tendency. Although the word 'convene' used by Dionysius has conciliar echoes (*synkalesas*), it seems that this was simply a conference for discussion (*koinologia*); however, it lasted three days, and succeeded in restoring Korakion, the leader of the sect, to orthodoxy.

I would emphasize the synodical character of this assembly, in which, contrary to the proceedings over Origen, each brother was allowed to express himself freely, before the primate, in a very ecclesial spirit of dialogue. Dionysius himself bears witness to this in a moving letter which Eusebius has preserved for us:

When I arrived in the district of Arsinoe, where as you know this notion (of Nepos) had long been widely held, so that schisms and secesions of entire churches had taken place, I called a meeting of the presbyters and teachers of the village congregations, with any laymen who wished to attend, and urged them to thrash out the question in public . . . I sat with them three days on end from dawn to dusk, trying to correct what had been written. In the process I was immensely impressed by the essential soundness, complete sincerity, logical grasp and mental clarity shown by these good people, as we methodically and good-temperedly dealt with questions, objections and points of agreement . . . There was no shirking of difficulties, but to the limit of our powers we tried to grapple with the problems and master them; nor were we too proud, if worsted in argument, to abandon our position and admit defeat: conscientiously, honestly, and with simple-minded trust in God, we accepted the conclusions to be drawn from the proofs and teachings of holy scripture (HE 7, 24, 6–8).

This form of mutual help in the orthodox faith perfectly reflects the meetings which Origen himself had arranged some years earlier, between 238 and 244, to restore Bishop Beryllus to orthodoxy at Bostra, and then, between 244 and 249, to enlighten Heraclides on the faith.[7] Eusebius calls them synods, and here Origen uses language showing that such a discussion is the concern of the whole ecclesial community. After the bishops present have expounded their points of view, and Heraclides himself has spelt out his form of belief, he speaks 'with the permission of God, the bishops, the priests and the faithful', and adds: 'All the church is listening. There must be no difference between churches on doctrine, for you are not the church of the lie.'

In the fourth century, several important synods took place in Alexandria, but in the majority of cases we do not have their acts. However, the circumstances in which they were convened, and the letters published after their sessions, are revealing evidence about the Egyptian synodical tradition.

In 306, after the great persecution, Peter of Alexandria presided at a 'joint synod of bishops' to depose Meletius for being both apostate and schismatic.[8] Fifteen years later, after long attempts to restore the priest Arius to a more authentic view of the faith, Alexander of Alexandria felt constrained to convene an assembly of around a hundred bishops. The Greek term used here is *synedrion*, a synonym for synod, but with the connotations of a tribunal. The condemnation of the heretic and his supporters was notified in a letter sent to all the churches, many of which responded by expressing their agreement in writing. In 324 the primate sent another letter to put bishops 'abroad' on their guard against Arian doctrines. He also invited them to support him by sending him a similar declaration to that of all the bishops 'of Egypt and the Thebaid, of Libya and the Pentapolis, and of Syria, Lycia, Pamphylia, Asia, Cappadocia and other distant provinces which have written to us against the Arians and have subscribed to our dossier'. The same year, another synod was held, again at Alexandria, to depose the priest Colluthus, who had allowed himself to ordain other priests.

Under the long episcopate of Athanasius (328–373), a series of councils was again held at Alexandria. Those known to us date for the most part from the period when the bishop was restored to his community on return from exile.[9]

After his first exile in 338, Athanasius brought together about a hundred bishops from Egypt, Libya, the Thebaid and Pentapolis to refute the accusations made against him. A little later, around the middle of 339, he wrote an 'encyclical letter' to the bishops of the entire world, 'his brothers in office in every place'. Immediately on his return from his second exile, in 346, he convened an Egyptian synod in order to emphasize that he was in accord with more than 400 bishops of all countries. Ten years later, again having been expelled, he wrote an 'encyclical letter to the bishops of Egypt and Libya' to put them on guard against the heretics.

The famous 'synod of the confessors' was held in 362 on Athanasius' return from his third exile. Although it brought together only twenty-one bishops, it was to have great influence. It was concerned with the reconciliation of converted heretics and the doctrine of the Holy Spirit. It gave rise to the famous synodical letter known as the 'Tome to the Antiochenes'. After his fourth very brief exile, the primate of Alexandria convened yet another synod, in 363; its letter, addressed to the new emperor, Jovian, stated the faith of Nicaea.

During the last years of his pontificate, which had happily become calmer after a fifth exile, Athanasius again convened an important synod, in 369 or 370. In the name of the ninety bishops of Egypt and Libya who had met together, he composed a 'letter to the bishops of Africa' to warn them against Arian arguments. He called on them to remain true to the faith of the church, since 'the word of the Lord handed down through the ecumenical synod of Nicaea will abide for ever' (PG 26, 1032B–C).

This series of Alexandrian councils which extends through the fourth century shows the effort made by the Egyptian churches to preserve the unity of the faith. In the wake of small local synods in which there was brotherly discussion for mutual enlightenment, aimed at a better understanding of doctrine, important regional synods regularly brought together a number of bishops, anxious to be unanimous in keeping to the message of Christ. In expressing their fidelity here, the bishops were aware of their solidarity with all the churches, and indeed this solidarity was their concern. That explains the existence of the numerous so-called 'ecumenical' letters, sent not only to all the bishops of Egypt and the various African countries but also to the bishops of the whole world. The synodicality which was exercised here locally was never divorced from catholicity.

The notion of sister churches, which we already find in II John 13 and which is mentioned in Cappadocia by St Basil,[10] is not at all strange to Africa. We find it stated by Synesius, bishop of Cyrene from 410 to 414. Courageously, he excommunicated the prefect Andronicus, whose use of torture made a mock of human rights; he then went on to write to his fellow bishops to warn them and to invite them to respect his decision. His letter, which is not well known but is a very fine one, ends with these words: 'This is what the church of Ptolemais asks of its sisters: that no temple of God be open to Andronicus and his people, to Thoas and his people . . . If some think that we are not much of a church, the church of a small and poor village, and if, without taking heed of our orders, they welcome those whom we have excommunicated, let them be aware that they are tearing apart the church of God which Christ wills to be one' (PG 66, 1401C).

III The age of Donatism and Pelagianism: Aurelius and Augustine

The period for which we have most documentation about African synodical practice is beyond question that of Donatism and Pelagianism, when the two great figures of Aurelius and Augustine stand out. Their long episcopates coincided, the former at Carthage (391–430) and the latter at Hippo (395–430).[11]

Before them, we know of only three Catholic councils in North Africa during the fourth century. The first, which was held at Cirta in Numidia, probably in the spring of 307, was a gathering of eleven bishops who met to elect one of their number, Silvanus, to the see of Cirta. They were led to examine their consciences together and to reveal that all had been 'traitors'.[12] More important was the general council which took place at Carthage in 348 or 349, which had been prepared for by provincial synods. The way in which Gratus spoke at it is typical of the synodical spirit of the African churches: a concern for dialogue and peace, in fidelity to the will of God and the scriptures:

It is by the will of God that we are assembled in the cause of unity: we have celebrated councils in the different provinces, and it is from these different provinces of Africa that today we have come to Carthage for our council. So deliberate with My Lowliness; let us discuss the essential points in connection with which we need to remind ourselves of the divine precepts and the teaching of the holy scriptures, to consider our time of unity, and on each of these points to take a decision of such a kind that Carthage does not diminish the vigour of the law, yet we do not make a ruling which is too severe in this age of unity.[13]

But Donatism was still far from being extinguished. Given the magnitude of the drama, the Catholics were to renew their efforts for unity. Under Genethlius, a new general council took place in Carthage on 16 June 390, with a limited number of participants. After expounding the orthodox doctrine of the Trinity, it took disciplinary measures, five of which related to bishops. Canon 12 in particular requires that a bishop shall not be ordained without consultation with the metropolitan, i.e. the primate of the province.

It is with Aurelius, elected to the see of Carthage in 391, that African conciliar life resumes a more intense rhythm. The new primate convened no less than thirty councils during his forty years as bishop, firmly supported in this by Augustine. Hardly had Augustine been ordained priest than he wrote to Aurelius to encourage him to 'purge the church of Africa from the excesses and stains which it suffers in many of its members and which so few bewail . . . According to the holy scriptures it is important to seek to cure this plague which a degenerate and licentious freedom has brought upon the church.' To achieve that, Augustine suggests that in particular the practice of synods should be revived: 'It is true that the contagion of this evil has made so much progress that in my view only the authority of a council is capable of curing it' (*Ep*. 22.2, 4). Perhaps it was because of this personal intervention that the first assembly to be convened and presided over by Aurelius of Carthage should have taken place at Hippo. This was a 'plenary council of all Africa', held on 3 October 393. At the request of the bishops, Augustine, a simple priest, preached at it on the faith and the creed.[14]

This adjective 'plenary' recurs very often – about forty times – in the writings of the bishop of Hippo. It is sometimes even applied to a provincial council. However, most often it denotes a wider assembly (*concilium universale*), perhaps one of all the provinces of North Africa (*concilium Africae*, or *totius Africae*), perhaps one that brings together the bishops from several continents (*totius orbis*, or *totius orbis christiani*). In the African vocabulary of the time, then, it is necessary to distinguish three kinds of council: the provincial council, the council of all Africa (from Mauritania to Tripolitania), and the council with a more universal character. However, the local assemblies and those which deliberate on the choice of a bishop are also synodical.

In the decisions of the council of 397 one can discern the growing role of the primate of Carthage, who fixes the date of Easter and gives his consent to the establishment of primates of the African provinces. We should note above all the decision taken to convene the general council of Africa annually. The provinces were to be represented by three bishops each, with the exception of Tripolitania, so small that it would only send one delegate. This prescription is important, because it shows the concern in North Africa to act permanently in a synodical fashion. Canon 8 of the Council of North Africa of 401 confirms that. But difficulties over travelling and the financial burdens of such meetings led the council in 407 to stipulate that from then on the councils would take place only when the need was felt to take counsel over a 'matter of common interest, i.e. one concerning all Africa' (canon 95); other questions were left to be dealt with by the province concerned. However, while Aurelius and Augustine remained alive, the general assemblies continued to be frequent – almost twenty in all.

At this time, in fact, the Donatist schism was the main problem. A solution had to be found to it at all costs, so that the unity and peace of the church could be re-established. That explains the abundance of councils between 393 and 411, despite the difficult circumstances which often hindered the assemblies. Leaving aside Donatist synods, which were frequent and well attended, this period has left traces of the convening of sixteen catholic councils – almost one a year –, eleven of them plenary, as well as the famous 'Conference of Carthage' in 411 with its 565 bishops: 286 catholic and 279 Donatist. This frequency is the sign of a clear concern to tackle the problems of the time together, to reflect on them and to respond in an agreed perspective.

The way in which the bishops express themselves bears witness to this. Thus the council of 401 is aware of its bond with Pope Anastasius of Rome, whose charity is 'paternal and fraternal', and who has 'such a pious concern for the members of Christ, who, though fixed in different regions, are established in the unity of one body'. As the council fathers continue, 'We take our decisions after considering and examining attentively all that would seem to us to be in the interests of the church, as this is indicated and inspired by the Spirit of God.'[15] However, their decision to welcome converted Donatist priests as priests – because of an acute lack of pastors at this time – was contrary to that of the Council of Rome, the validity of which the fathers recognized.

The unity of the members of the council appears again in the fact that they consider that they form a 'fraternity'.[16] Similarly, the spirit of charity towards the Donatists indicates the concern for peace which motivates them. So the invitation sent to them in 403 to participate in a free discussion between the representatives of the two rival churches with a view to re-establishing religious unity in Africa is typical. 'God has warned by the prophet that we should say "You are our brothers" (II Sam. 19.13) even to those who declare that they are not our brothers. So you should not scorn our warning, given in peace and motivated by charity, that if you think that you possess any truth, you should not hesitate to show it.'[17]

During the Pelagian period, too (411–427), councils followed one another with impressive frequency. Between 411 and 416 we know of at least sixteen, six of which were plenary. 217 bishops took part in that of May 419. The series was interrupted by the Vandal invasions. In addition to the concern shared with Innocent I, the problem of Pelagianism, the councils of this period often dealt with disciplinary questions. It was in connection with these that there was some tension between Africa and Rome at the time. Following the intrigue of Celestius with Pope Zosimus, the council of 418 allowed an appeal to the primate of the province, or even to the plenary synod of Carthage, but not to Rome. There was renewed tension when the excommunicated priest Apiarius was well received by Zosimus, and relations deteriorated further when Pope Celestine admitted him to communion. At that point the plenary council of 424 sent a synodical letter to the pope asking him to stop intervening and to respect the principle of subsidiarity.[18]

We should note that these synods did not deal only with faith and discipline. They also touched on questions of society and justice, as is evident from the letters of Augustine recently discovered by Divjak. For example, the synod of May 419 set up a commission to reflect on specific current problems, which two delegates were then to discuss with the emperor. They were to ask him for clemency following disturbances at Carthage caused by an overwhelming burden of taxation and petitioned him to pass a law guaranteeing clearly and effectively the right of sanctuary in churches. Some months later, a provincial council of Numidia made an approach of the same kind, supported by Augustine, who suggested that the civil authorities should reinstate the institution of 'defenders' of the common people in cities to protect the weak against the greed, injustice and corruption of the powerful, in particular in connection with the redistribution of taxes. Around 422 it again intervened to ask for action against the trade in slaves and children for forced labour.[19]

In the sixth century, after the Vandal invasions, another four plenary councils were held: at Hadrumeta in 507, at Carthage on 5 and 6 February 525 with sixty bishops, and in 534 with 220 bishops, who issued three synodical letters: we also know of four provincial councils. Though the number of assemblies was less than before, we can still see the formation of canonical collections. The *Breviarium hipponense* was produced as early as 397. Then came the *Codex canonum Ecclesiae africanae* of the council of 419, to which was added the *codex Apiarii causae*. Then, around 680–90, there was the long *Corcordia Canonum* of the African bishop Cresconius.[20] At a time when the communities had become too weak to meet, these compilations made it possible at least to preserve the principal fruit of the synodical work of the first African churches.

Conclusion

Rapid though the survey which we have just made has been, it shows clearly that synodical practice is a characteristic of the church of Christ. In Africa, as everywhere else during the first centuries, it was very developed from the beginning. Particularly important documentation for Egypt and above all for North Africa is evidence of this. The frequency of the synods themselves is already a sign. Although there were no so-called 'ecumenical' councils, we can note that the churches came together to discover better from the scriptures, and under the inspiration of the Spirit, how to live out the ecclesial tradition in response to the needs of the communities in each place and of each period.

The local church reflects in common on its various problems: the deepening of its faith, the choice of its ministers, the organization of its way of life. But it always does so in communion with the neighbouring churches. That gives rise to the custom of provincial synods and then, more broadly, to the regional assemblies of North Africa or Egypt. These 'plenary' meetings are never felt to be cut off from more distant regions: communion with these regions is shown by the sending of synodical or encyclical letters. When the need for wider councils, bringing together delegates from all over the Christian world, is felt, Africans take part in them.

The purpose of these councils is not just to resolve particular problems. Above all they are prompted by a concern for unity: to maintain communion within a community round its bishop, unity between sister churches of the same region, and concord with the one church which is alive in all the countries of the world. *Koinonia* is the fundamental ecclesial reality which has to be safeguarded and developed, without denying either the principle of subsidiarity or a certain diversity.

Concretely, these assemblies often study the problems of faith, above all in the face of certain major heresies like Arianism and Pelagianism. But often, too, the risk or the presence of a schism explains why assemblies are convened: how could one remain inactive in the face of the divisions caused by the Novatians, the Meletians or the Donatists? However, orthodoxy is not the sole preoccupation of the councils. The discipline of the Christian life is also related to the authenticity of the gospel. Whether the issue is admission to the sacraments or the organization of the communities, everything has to be studied in synod. And when the emperor claimed to be a Christian, the assembled bishops had the courage to convey to him the demands of the gospel, which needed to be expressed in the civil laws.

As can be seen, what is striking here is not only the existence of the synod but the synodical spirit which inspires the church of Africa. It seems to have been especially developed at times of greatest difficulty, but it is shown above all among those bishops who are most concerned about the quality of life in their communities. We should not think, however, that synodical practice was limited to periods of crisis. While crises may in fact have prompted many assemblies which were important enough to have their writings preserved, we must suppose that many other synods took place, particularly at provincial level, even if we have no traces of them. History suggests this, and many recent studies, or even the discovery of new documents, prove it.

This should not surprise us. The existence and development of the councils is the normal fruit of the life of the church, which is aware that it is one in its legitimate diversity, and wants to have that character, because it is 'brotherhood' in Christ.[21] That is why it is always seeking the will of the Lord, aware of the problems of its time and faithful to the gospel message. It constantly wants to realize as well as possible this unanimity given by the Spirit to those who are open to communal reflection in dialogue and sharing.

The church which is *synodia* and *synodos* can only live and grow in this spirit of synodicality of which the churches of Africa gave us such a fine example during the first centuries. There is no doubt that the Holy Spirit, still very much alive, will continue to guide the church today.

Translated by John Bowden

Notes

1. For the history of the words 'council' and 'synod' see the articles by A. Lumpe, *AnnHistConc* 1970, 1–21, and 1974, 40–53.
2. J. A. Fischer, 'Die ersten Konzilien im römischen nordwest-Afrika', in *Pietas*, Münster 1980, 217–27.
3. For Cyprian's councils see the articles by J. A. Fischer, *AnnHistConc* 1979, 263–86; 1981, 1–11, 12–26; 1982, 227–40; 1983, 1–14; 1984, 1–39, 243–53; *Zeitschrift für Kirchengeschichte*, 1982, 223–39; P. A. Aidon, 'The Procedure of St Cyprian's Synods', *Vigiliae Christianae*, 1983, 328–39.
4. CSEL III.1, 435–6.
5. In H. Legrand, *Les conférences episcopales*, Paris 1988, 53–84.
6. J. A. Fischer, 'Die Synode zu Alexandrien im Jahr 306', *AnnHistConc* 1987, 62–70.
7. Sources Chrétiennes 67: for the presence of the faithful cf. pp. 18–19.
8. J. A. Fischer, 'Werden und Eigenart der Konzilsidee des Athanasius von Alexandrien', in *Die Konzilsidee der Alten Kirche*, Paderborn 1979, 25–67.
9. Cf. H. J. Sieben, 'Werden und Elgenart der Konzilsidee des Athanasius von Alexandrien', in *Die Konzilsidee der Alten Kirche*. Paderborn 1979, 25–67.
10. Cf. E. Lanne, 'Eglises-soeurs', *Istina* 1975, 47–75; 'Eglise soeur et Eglise mère dans le vocabulaire de l'Eglise ancienne', *Communion sanctorum*, 1982, 86–97.
11. H. J. Sieben, 'Konzilien in Leben und Lehre des Augustinus von Hippo', in *Die Konzilsidee* (n. 9), 68–102.
12. J. A. Fischer, 'Das kleine Konzil zu Cirta im Jahr 305 (?)', *AnnHistConc* 1986, 281–92.
13. Cf. J. -L. Maier, *Le Dossier du Donatisme* I, Berlin 1987, 291–6.

14. G. Bardy, 'Conciles d'Hippone au temps de saint Augustin', *Augustiniana* 1955, 451–8.

15. Cf. Maier, *Dossier* (n. 13), II, 1989, 111–16.

16. CCL 149, 205f.

17. Maier, *Dossier* (n. 13), II, 1989, 122–3.

18. For this theme cf. C. Munier, 'Un canon inédit du XXe concile de Carthage', *Revue des Sciences Religieuses*, 1966, 113–26.

19. M. -F. Berrouard, 'Un tournant dans la vie de l'Eglise d'Afrique', *Revue des Etudes Augustiniennes*, 1985, 46–70.

20. *Concilia Africae A.345– A.525*, CCSL 149; C. Munier, 'La tradition littéraire des canons africains (345–525)', *Recherches Augustiniennes*, 1975, 3–22; J. Gaudemet, *Les sources du droit de l'Eglise en Occident*, Paris 1985, 79–83, 137–9.

21. Cf. M. Dujarier, *L'Eglise-Fraternité*, Paris 1991.

II · The Most Striking Christian Experiences in the African Churches between Vatican II and the African Synod

The Birth and Development of a Local Church: Difficulties and Signs of Hope

Elochukwu E. Uzukwu

I The agony of the birth of a local church

The church in Africa was *born old*.[1] The midwives expected it and the old child really had no choice. Thus from the time of the missionary preaching up to Vatican II and beyond, structures like places of worship, primary, secondary and catechetical schools, seminaries, convents and hospitals, sprouted as both arms and results of evangelization. What was foremost in the mind of the evangelizers was to establish a church; and, naturally, West European church structures were transplanted. The effects of this missionary impact on Africa were remarkable. A glance at the statistics compiled by Barrett shows a steady growth of Christians (including Roman Catholics), especially between 1900 and 1970.[2]

The successors whom the missionaries appointed continued their strategy and shepherded the flock. But being schooled in prudential compliance to authority and tradition, they lacked initiative. The desire expressed by the late Cardinal Malula in 1959 for a truly African church in an independent African country was more an exception than the rule. Church leaders were operating in a feudalistic institution very much concerned with power. It appears to me that this inherited pre-Vatican II feudal image of the church constitutes the greatest obstacle to the emergence of dynamic local churches in Africa.

The Second Vatican Council broke through this authority-conscious model of church and projected the image of the *people of God*. A basic equality exists! Each member is called to holiness, called to participate fully in the life of the church; and ministry is exercised for the good of the body of Christ. This new vision of church encouraged local churches in Africa to initiate actions responding to local needs. For example, in Zaire the liturgy was seen to be foreign to the context; ministry needed to be applied in a different way (*bakambi* – lay leadership); and theology had to respond to the African context. But the authority structure in the church would make the birth of a *local* church very difficult. The experiment of small Christian communities (SCCs) in East Africa will bring this out.

The church in East Africa functioning under the umbrella of the Association of Member Episcopal Conferences of Eastern Africa (AMECEA) resolved to evolve a more active and responsive church – self-ministering, self-propagating and self-supporting. To ensure dynamic witness as church right from the grass roots level, AMECEA decided to establish SCCs as from 1976. Ten years later (1986), an evaluation of SCCs noted some achievements. However, the project did not attain its overall purpose. It has not been operative in many dioceses; and, where it operated, its 'major problems' are linked to clerical resistance and control:

> Some dioceses have done little to encourage SCCs in practical terms . . . SCCs are clerical-centred with little and at times no initiative at all from the laity . . . Some priests fear that if such communities are not properly managed other sects may spring up. There has been over-supervision of the SCCs due to fears of the dangers of the emergence of 'splinter groups' and 'schisms' . . . Thus SCC leaders are not allowed to take full responsibility . . . Other people do not like changes. They want to continue things as they always did . . . When the laity are responsible the clergy tend to be very strict. Good recommendations from the Christian communities are not welcome.[3]

The new style of being church (SCC) results from the breath of the Spirit, but its application lies in the hands of those who exercise authority in the church. This new style threatens the command structure; those in power are not ready for change. AMECEA saw initiative and responsibility as fundamental to the emergence of a dynamic local church; but these must be supervised and even must originate from the clergy in order to ensure right doctrine and right practice. One agrees that preserving right doctrine and practice (Titus 1.19; 2.1) is a value to be maintained in the church; care must also be taken to control those with itching ears (II Tim. 4.3) for novelties. But in the SCC experiment this fear of novelties appears to have been exaggerated. The problems of the SCC are part of the burden of European Christianity which the African clergy appears unwilling to cast off. The pyramidal pattern of ecclesiastical administration ensures that the bishops are the extension of the pope, the priests are the extension of the bishop, and the laity are the extension of the priest.

The consequences of this practice are devastating for both the church and the Black race. The church's ministry (*diakonia*, Mark 10.45) equips it to introduce the 'leaven' (change) into society from the grass roots; but because of its outmoded command structure, the church is running the risk of playing the role of spectator in the present drama of life in Africa, a drama which may determine the future of the continent and the role of the Black race in the global village. Maintaining this ideology of authority in its training programme, the church persists in shielding candidates for the priesthood and religious life from the concern of life in Africa; and thus for the foreseeable future ministers in the church may *be* in Africa but not *live* in Africa. The major concern in Africa today is *hunger*. In Nigeria, for example, people struggle to beat a neo-colonialist politico-economic arrangement in order to survive. But the issue in the church is *power*. Among the qualities required to function as a good priest or religious, obedience comes out on top. In a continent where 50% live in absolute poverty, and an estimated 400 million (according to the United Nations Development Programme) will be living in extreme poverty by 1995,[4] candidates for the priesthood and religious life are assured of food and other material necessities of life by foreign agencies and the local contribution of the laity. They are thus rendered incapable of appreciating in a practical way the lot of a majority of Africans; also the root cause of our poverty escapes them at a practical level. However, they are *dependent* because they *are fed*. But instead of abandoning the dependency syndrome by directing attention to the concern of Africa, they are diverted by the finger that feeds them to be preoccupied with the concerns of the church of Rome – its laws, its rituals, its doctrines: these are imposed on a bemused mass of believers, whether they are tangentially related to contextual problems or not.

A conference like AMECEA has instinctively put its finger on the solution to the problem of the local churches in Africa – grass-roots mobilization. It thus decided that the 'systematic formation of small Christian communities should be the key pastoral priority in Eastern Africa'.[5] However, the church in Africa has to go one step further. It has to reform its leadership structures. In traditional Africa, before the colonial dictatorship, two political systems were prevalent: concentration of authority in the hands of one man (the king assisted by his council), and the dispersal of authority in community (or direct democracy: leadership in the hands of heads of families, kindreds and associations). In these two systems, despite abuses, leadership is preferred to rulership.[6] Leadership is also the controlling idea of ministry in the various churches of the New Testament which the apostles left behind. No matter how centralized a New Testament church may be (e.g. the church of the Pastoral Letters),[7] feudalistic structures are unheard of. The church in Africa should allow itself to be influenced both by the traditional political systems and by the New Testament experience to assume proper patterns of ministry. Today the need for the church to give leadership in Africa has become more urgent. In a continent where authority is expressed in terms of arrogant exercise of power, the church in Africa is called upon to present an alternative pattern of building community. It must break with feudalism in order to allow the grass-roots communities like the small Christian communities to assume their responsibilities as church.

Signs of hope

In many parts of Africa, national episcopal conferences have celebrated the centenary of evangelization. Despite the birth pangs outlined above, maturation, though difficult, is in progress. The courageous decision by AMECEA to establish SCCs has made some communities acquire the experience of reflecting on the word and applying it to their social context. Local patterns have also been acquired in catechetics and liturgy in AMECEA countries. The primary position given to inculturation by the Zairean conference has led to the development of aspects of consecrated life, pastoral, liturgy and theology. Inculturation in this region should not be measured simply by the 'Roman Missal for the Dioceses of Zaire'. In this direction the Cameroonian mass, the rite of Christian initiation in Burkina Faso, the Christian marriage rite in Chad, and so on, are experiences giving local characteristics to the church. The trauma of post-independence Africa made national and regional conferences take positions against military dictatorships, ethnic and religious intolerance, poverty and oppression. The Symposium of Episcopal Conferences of Africa and Madagascar favours integral human promotion as evangelization and criticizes the infringement of human rights. The five Catholic faculties of theology now functioning in Africa are expected to make the African local experience the starting point of their theological reflection. All these are signs of hope of an evolving local church. They will help to demarcate this local church in so far as the church leadership courageously embraces the freedom of the children of God, since catholicity implies diversity and unity.

Other signs of hope lie in an area not immediately under the control of the church hierarchy. I suggest that just as the issue of power provides the key to the difficulties of our local churches, so also the confidence the Christian *people* repose in their local (ancestral) experience may indicate the way forward.

In Nigeria, and generally all over Africa, the phenomenon of the search for security or for integral well-being has today assumed unprecedented dimensions. Christians of all denominations, Muslims and practitioners of traditional religion, rub shoulders at any healing centre (Catholic, Aladura, Muslim or traditional). The problems which drive them to such centres are rather mixed: sickness of all descriptions, infertility, fear of witchcraft and sorcery, progress in business enterprise, fear of armed robbers and secret societies, and so on. The widespread benefits of modern life (Western technology, education and medicine) and the insistent teaching of Christianity are unable to arrest such a rush. Rather, patterns of response to this hunger for integral well-being are developing into an authoritative tradition of experience. This movement may rightly be interpreted as folk religion. However, from the evidence in the field[8] we appear to be witnessing not simply folk religion but rather the preference for a framework of interpreting reality different from the received Western Christian one. This framework, based on the authority of ancestral experience, locates human beings firmly in the cosmos and insists that their integral well-being is the ultimate reality and meaning. To realize this, the physical and spiritual dimensions of life in the cosmos (all of which become actual in human beings – the microcosm) must function harmoniously.[9] The vehicle of this ancestral experience is ancestral (African) religion. As a *religion of structure*, it introduces harmony/rhythm into everyday normal life. In it 'all energies are directed to the ritual sustenance of the normal order', i.e. 'as imbedded in norms going back to the beginning of time, and as usual and commonplace reality'. In this world-view, the social, economic, political, personal and cosmic dimensions of life are integrated (under the eyes of the gods). Experts in the various areas of endeavour increase the possibilities for community and individual to live an integral life.

The encounter with Christianity and modernity failed to satisfy the yearning of Africans for integral well-being. Specialization in the West informed by the Enlightenment and Cartesianism moves towards isolation and separation. The autonomy of each discipline is affirmed in total independence of other areas of human endeavour. Secularization limits religious practice (Christianity) to a particular area of human life.

A predictable conflict is thus being experienced by African Christians. The problem is not only how to convert a religion of salvation (Christianity) into a religion of structure but also how to make the benefits of modernity function in the holistic vision of the universe. The popular African Christian solution is that faith in Christ brings healing (christo-therapy). In other words, the guarantor of security, the anchor which ensures harmony in the cosmos (God-Christ), must heal bodies as well as spirit. Health and medicine function under the eyes of God-Christ (integration). Modernity and religion are complementary.

The decision by many African Christians to search for integration in their world is a way of insisting that life in the cosmos, instead of moving towards the separation or isolation of levels and components, is moving towards relation and harmony. This is drawn from the authority of ancestral experience. As a viable framework of interpreting present reality it leaves itself open to criticism (and even contradiction) by the new situation. But today, what appears uppermost in the minds of people in Africa is the integral well-being of humankind (men and women). The authority of ancestral experience maintains its vigour in a changing world.

Many committed Christians believe that it is not necessary to return to ancestral religion to live an integral life. Their praxis insists that this core of the ancestral experience is a universal vision of man which is expressible in any religious tradition, including Christianity. Faith in Christ, instead of being diminished, is rather complemented by the ancestral experience. Pastors in the field are trying to catch up with Christians who, trusting their experience, have moved ahead. It is at this crucial point, where Christians decide to trust their experience and forward-looking pastors are compelled to change their practice in order to respond to the reality of the Christian life in Africa, that I see a central sign of hope for Christianity in Africa.

It is important to insist that ordinary lay Catholics with *normal problems of life* in Africa took the initiative in resolving their life-problems. The pastors who learn from their experiences are privileged to re-examine in a practical way the meaning of salvation in Christ for the masses of African believers. For example, Fr G. Ikeobi (Nigeria) has developed not only a liturgy for healing but also rituals for peace among feuding villages, contract rituals among business associates, purification rituals following suicides, and many more. Frs E. Ede (Nigeria), M. Hebga (Cameroon), Bishop Milingo and many others devote most of their time to bringing a Christian response to 'normal' life-problems of the context. In this way the normal problems of the context challenge the received Christian faith and relevant answers are demanded.

On the whole, the experience of alienation in varying degrees by practising Catholics in Africa is a reality which the church cannot simply wish away. The responses proposed by courageous and charismatic pastors remain unco-ordinated on the level of the local church. Each pastor becomes an expert. Abuses are not wanting. A reformed church leadership in tune with problems of the context has to direct its attention to this hunger for integral well-being. The commitment to inculturation should apply to all dimensions of life; and the integral well-being of humankind as realized in each context would become its guiding principle. Theological reflection which has integral well-being of men and women as its focal point will employ this framework to reinterpret the whole Christian experience and propose ways for its practice in the various facets of life in contemporary African society. In this way the full force of the message of Christ may stimulate African life today because of its consonance with Africa's hunger for integral well-being.

Notes

1. O. Bimwenyi-Kweshi, 'Religions Africaines, un "lieu" de la Théologie Chrétienne africaine', in *Religions Africaines et Christianisme. Colloque International de Kinshasa, 9–14 January 1978*, Kinshasa 1979, Vol. II, 168.

2. D. B. Barrett (ed.), *World Christian Encyclopedia*, Nairobi 1982, p. 782.

3. J. G. Healey, 'Four Africans Evaluate SCCs in E. Africa', *African Ecclesial Review* 29.5, 1987, 266–77.

4. P. Gifford, *Christianity: To Save or Enslave?*, Harare: Ecumenical Documentation and Information Centre of Eastern and Southern Africa 1990, 1.

5. AMECEA Bishops, 'Guidelines for the Catholic Church in Eastern Africa in the 1980s', *African Ecclesial Review* 16.1, 2, 1974, 9–10.

6. M. Fortes and E. E. Evans-Pritchard, *African Political Systems*, London 1940.

7. R. E. Brown, *The Churches the Apostles Left Behind*, New York 1984.

8. *Healing and Exorcism – the Nigerian Experience. Acts of the First Missiology Symposium of the Spiritan International School of Theology, Enugu, 18–20 May 1989* (ready for publication); E. Milingo, *The World in Between*, Ibadan 1986; M. P. Hegba, *Sorcellerie et Prière de Délivrance*, Paris 1982.

9. E. M. Zeusse, *Ritual Cosmos. The Sanctification of Life in African Religions*, Athens, Ohio 1979, 3f.

Church and Society in Lusophone Africa

Francisco Joâo Silota

Our missionary vocation 'to propagate the faith and the empire' continues overseas.[1]

I should start by confessing that my theme is very wide both geographically and in content. Geographically, because it includes all the Lusophone countries in Africa. In content, because one has to show what the church has been doing in different aspects of society in those countries: religion, school education, health, culture, economics, etc. This cannot be done in a short article. That is why I shall speak in very general terms and with special reference to Mozambique.

Second, the subject is very embarrassing for me because, as can be seen in the quotation above, there has been a certain ambiguity in the action of the church in the ex-Portuguese colonies. So, anyone wanting to state things as they happened might be accused of resentment and a tendency to blame the past. That is not my intention.

Third, if I am to be understood, I ought to give some background to the subject, even summarily.

1. According to what we can gather from history, Lusophone Africa has been in contact with the message of the gospel since the first half of the fifteenth century.[2] However, it was during the second half of the sixteenth century that some sort of a systematic evangelization started in ex-Portuguese Africa: the Jesuits were among the pioneers, especially in Angola and Mozambique.[3]

After a long period with several crises, evangelization gained ground at the end of the last century. But it only made firm progress with the concordat and the missionary agreement between Portugal and the Holy See in 1940.

2. According to the concordat and the missionary agreement, the freedom of the church in its apostolic field was not only recognized but also guaranteed by the state.[4] However, there was a sort of *quid pro quo* in this agreement. For while on the one hand the church was given all privileges and honours, on the other hand some of its specific activities were restricted. There was, for instance, the case of articles 9 and 10 of the missionary statute which specified that the residential bishops, vicar general, apostolic administrator and persons in charge of any church institution should be Portuguese citizens. Moreover, no nomination of an archbishop or bishop could be made without consulting the state, which had to see whether there would be any political objections.[5] In spite of all that, the concordat and missionary agreement gave rise to a new missionary impetus. First, because the ecclesiastical hierarchy was altered in all the ex-Portuguese colonies, Guinea was separated from the diocese of Santiago de Cabo Verde and made a mission in its own right. Angola and Mozambique were promoted to ecclesiastical provinces, with three dioceses created in each of them.[6] The same factor also contributed greatly to the influx of the missionaries of several orders into these countries.

Triumphalistically enthusiastic about the concordat, fair, perhaps without foreseeing its negative implications, the then Patriarch of Lisbon, the late Cardinal Cerejeira, was to say:

> Never till this day has the Holy See signed such a vast and such a transcendent statute about the missionary regime (. . .). The person who has felt the keenness of the colonial chess-board and, especially if he is a Christian soul, responsibility for the salvation of indigenous souls who, as it was said in the sixteenth century, must be won over (conquered) for Christ and his church, will be able to grasp the scope of the agreement which has just been signed. Our missionary vocation 'to propagate the Faith and the Empire' continues overseas.[7]

One just wonders how both the Holy See and the Patriarch of Lisbon could not see the danger involved in all this. As a matter of fact, using the advantage it had obtained over the church, months later the state issued the following statement:

> The overseas Portuguese Catholic missions are regarded as institutions of imperial usefulness and of great civilizing scope.[8]

This article of the missionary statute, which was also accepted by the church, revealed the whole intention of the Portuguese government behind the concordat and the agreement. They gave all sorts of privileges to the church so as subtly to use it later on for their imperial purposes. In this, Salazar's regime seems to have perceived clearly that our holy mother church is made up of human beings and, therefore, corruptible. As a matter of fact, it was not long before the popular saying was confirmed: 'power corrupts'. Seeing themselves with such privileges and honours in their apostolic activities, many missionaries, especially Portuguese, wanting to show gratitude to such a 'magnanimous' state, would try to reconcile what the gospel declared incompatible (Matt. 6.24). They wanted to serve two masters by being agents of the spread of both the faith and the empire.

> However, as we spread the faith, it is concomitantly our wish to spread the empire as well, for we are interested in everything that concerns the development and progress of this colony, as we kindle in souls the sacred fire of love of God and of the fatherland.[9]

3. This obvious contradictory attitude had indeed been the practical and general leitmotif for a good number of Portuguese missionaries. Indeed, it came into being as a legacy from the very first days of Portugal's discoveries, as is witnessed by the greatest epic in the Portuguese world, *The Lusiads*. In it, Luis de Camoes, as he sings the wonders of Portugal, speaks of 'spreading the faith and the empire'.[10] So, many Portuguese missionaries in the overseas dominions saw themselves as the bearers of both Portuguese civilization and the message of the gospel. More astonishing still, very often some of them would give priority to the former. That meant that the people in the overseas dominions had first to assimilate the Portuguese way of life in order to receive the message of the gospel in Portuguese culture.

> Instruction posts will be created to teach the native to speak Portuguese and to pray like Portuguese people.
>
> The posts might be fixed or moveable, as the administrator might see it more convenient for the spreading of our language and our religion.
>
> The expenses of the instruction posts are met by the fund for assistance to natives under the rubric 'Diffusion of the Portuguese Language and the Religion of Portuguese People'.[11]

From this we see that the 'native' had to undergo spiritual, cultural, socio-economic, moral and religious assimilation. Through the church-state collaboration, people of the colonies had to lose their identity and authenticity in order to get school education and be Christian. This meant, in other words, that the church of Portugal was to have impeccable continuity in parts of the world with a completely different genius. 'To teach the native to pray like Portuguese people'! In the opinion of the late Patriarch of Lisbon, this religious absurdity showed the responsibility the Portuguese had for the salvation of the souls of the natives. These had by all means to be 'conquered' for Christ. But how would the Christ who never forced anybody to be his now accept those forced natives?

Nevertheless, in the words of the cardinal, since the Portuguese had a 'missionary vocation "to propagate the faith and the empire"', they felt it their duty to 'conquer the indigenous souls'. Thus it was only logical that, once conquered, the natives had to follow the way of life indicated by the conquerors. The right to their own culture and their own beliefs would not count any more.

The amazing thing is that this way of thinking, backed by the concordat, has been so deeply rooted in some minds that its after-effects are still felt in the church even after the Second Vatican Council.

> The theological arguments of our missionary vocation and the main lines of our pastoral action among lay people in order to involve them in the work for the missions are the following. The missionaries of the Holy Ghost are the vanguard of the empire. The Portuguese missionary follows along the road of this ideal: bearing Christ to the whole world and telling men what Portugal is.[12]

4. It was more or less in this atmosphere that political independence came to Lusophone Africa in the early 1970s. Admittedly, immediately after the Second Vatican Council there had been some moves towards an eventual incarnation of the gospel in local realities. But it was such a timid and rare initiative that it was hardly noticed. The general atmosphere, therefore, was that of a Portuguese church. Hence the words of the late President Samora:

> Religion, and in particular the Catholic church, has contributed a great deal to the cultural and human alienation of Mozambiquan man, making him a submissive tool and an object of exploitation, in order to block, in the name of Christian resignation, any manifestation of resistance. Behold the heritage that we get today. It is a heritage of misery, of social and economic backwardness, disease, nudity, famine, ignorance, which are prodigal fruits of the same tree called exploitation, that grew and lived side by side with colonialism.[13]

This being the picture that people had got of the Catholic church in Mozambique and, certainly, in other ex-Portuguese colonies as well, one can easily understand the attitude taken by the new government, especially in Mozambique and Angola, in relation to religion in general.

> The People's Republic of Mozambique is a lay state, in which exists an absolute separation between the state and the religious institutions.[14]

Whatever might have been the real reasons that led the politicians to take this stand, it has been the best solution, especially for the church. History has shown sufficiently that whenever the church was too attached to the civil or military governing powers, it ended up by being their servant. And the church in the new states would not like to repeat such mistakes.

The church has made a self-examination. She has examined her mission according to the divine plan and her missionary action in Mozambique in times past. She acknowledges that a valuable work has been done as well as mistakes made and attitudes formed which were not very evangelical . . . Animated with a new spirit, she has decisively plunged herself into a search for new forms by which to live the gospel more fully. That is why we opted for 'a church of the grassroots and of communion, a church-family, with mutual services, freely offered; a church right in the heart of the people, who take her as their own, well inserted in human realities, and playing the role of leaven in society'.[15]

5. What the bishops are doing here is just reiterating the option chosen years earlier in a National Pastoral Assembly, in which all the baptized Roman Catholilcs were represented: bishops, priests, men and women religious, and the lay people at large. This was two years after political independence. The church had had enough time to experience the new situation and to start questioning herself seriously. So the assembly was taken as an opportunity for a deep reflection and a search for new ways of being church, in order to respond to the real aspirations of the Mozambiquan people.

As we come out of a triumphalistic church, too attached to the constituted powers, into a simple and poor church, separated from the state, freed from false security, concerned with her internal renewal, we get the feeling of being on the way to a church of the grassroots and of communion, a church-family, with mutual services, freely offered, a church right in the heart of the people, who take her as their own, inserted in human realities and playing the role of leaven in the society.[16]

The National Pastoral Assembly of 1977 was the turning point for the Catholic church in Mozambique. From adopting an attitude of ambiguity and a degree of complicity in the cultural genocide of the dominated, it is now taking a clear stand, and siding with the weak and the poor. From being a church preoccupied with maintaining the Portuguese religio-cultural expression, it is turning to the local reality. The embryo of a new era is seen starting to take shape. A new ecclesiology is to be conceived. But where are we to find the ideal matrix for this important reality? If it is to make any sense to the Mozambiquan people, it has to be formed and born in an atmosphere of simplicity similar to that in which the Word was made flesh and was born.

Such a fact leads us to give a new impulse to the work of suscitating, animating and promoting the life of small communities so that this life can grow ever more in order to favour the initiative and responsibility of the people of God in the building up of the local church. (For, as a matter of fact) the dynamics of the actual world, which rejects passivity and is characterized by co-responsibility, participation and initiative, are an invitation of the Spirit to the church that is being called to enter in this process.

The growth of the communities in spontaneity and discernment of what they need, leads them to discover the value of the ministries, thus helping them to understand the novelty of I Corinthians 12 and its importance in the building up of the Christian community. In this way we tend towards a ministerial church, whose foundation is Christ, the servant; where each member assumes his responsibility, in a community of servants.[17]

Concretely, this participation of the whole people of God in building up the local church is meant to imply a recognition and acceptance of the charisms manifested in the members, followed by a respective distribution of services for the good of the community. Because, 'as members, they share a common dignity from their rebirth in Christ' (*Lumen Gentium* 32).

And if by the will of Christ some are made teachers, dispensers of mysteries, and shepherds on behalf of others, yet all share a true equality with regard to the dignity and to the activity common to all the faithful for the building up of the Body of Christ (*Lumen Gentium* 32).

6. It is in this atmosphere of the Christian communities in which the members try to build up a church family that there are expectations of the birth of a church with a meaningful gospel message for the people of Lusophone Africa. Admittedly, since the National Pastoral Assembly in Mozambique, every diocese, parish and small community has been doing its best to overcome the long-lasting social, religious and cultural alienation.

As a matter of fact, we realize that the Christian communities are growing in all the dioceses, especially since the National Pastoral Assembly; lay people are progressively assuming their responsibilities in the life of communities and in the exercise of ministries that are entrusted to them. We also notice in everybody the desire to deepen and witness to the faith, even with risk and sacrifice.[18].

This is just one of the concomitant stages of the struggle. The fact that lay people are assuming their responsibilities is a very good sign, but it is not the final proof of a positive outcome in the future. Admittedly, the desire to deepen the faith is almost half achieved. But we know that faith cannot really be deepened before people are able to express it with their own categories. Hence the importance of initiating people so that, while they are trying to overcome their alienation, they have to work hard both to find the essence of the gospel message and to look for new ways of expression which are proper to them. Only then can one start speaking optimistically of incarnation.

The exchange of experiences between communities and dioceses is contributing to a great deal of communion and incarnation of the church in this country.[19]

7. Is the church in Mozambique and anywhere in Lusophone Africa really incarnated now? This apparently simple question is difficult to answer. For it all depends on what we understand by incarnation. If we understand it as a total insertion in a human milieu with all its implications, then I would say 'no'. Both the church and the message it is to preach are still very far from such an incarnation. But if we understand incarnation as a process, the answer is surely 'yes'. For, as we saw above, in the case of Mozambique, since the National Pastoral Asssembly, throughout the country there has been an effort to integrate the church in actual reality. The church should not stand aloof, on the margin of the revolutionary situation in which the country found itself. Both in Mozambique and in other Lusophone African countries, in a way that is proper to her mission, it has since tried actively to accompany the reconstruction of the new nations, encouraging every member of the faithful to do the same.

Convinced that the revolutionary process that is going on in the country includes positive values stemming from the gospel, Christians, as citizens with full rights, should be engaged in several tasks for national reconstruction (GS 11) such as the struggle against famine, disease, ignorance, misery, etc., assuming the responsibility that is proper to them, in the creation of a society without inequalities.[20]

So the church is no longer only concerned with the 'salvation of souls' but also with the integral well-being of each human being and of all society. It cannot be indifferent to the sufferings of people who are starving; of those feeling humiliated in their nudity; of those undergoing all sorts of exploitation because of ignorance and fear which are not their own fault; of those who find themselves psychologically torn because of a war whose causes they never knew, and whose consequences have been the loss of innocent lives. On the contrary, the church is trying to be present, as much as it possibly can, in all these situations. And it was precisely with this intention that throughout ex-Portuguese Africa it opted for establishing a dialogue with the government authorities and all men of good will so as to see how better they could collaborate in order to alleviate the overall misery that is devastating the countries.

8. It is clear that the church is using all the means at its disposal to serve people in their integrality. It is doing its best to make its own 'the joys and hopes, the griefs and anxieties, of men of this age, especially those who are poor or in any way afflicted' (GS 1). In Mozambique, through the National Commission of Caritas, it has been contributing a great deal to the agricultural schemes to alleviate hunger. It has been supplying school materials to diminish ignorance. It has been furnishing hospitals with medicine to fight against disease. More than that, it has courageously been playing a prophetic role: denouncing injustices and defending human rights, especially through pastoral letters.[21]

So we have to admit that socially, economically and even pastorally the church is working wonders throughout ex-Portuguese Africa. However, we have also to accept that this enormous endeavour of the church is not enough in itself for the incarnation and growth of the gospel in these countries. There is another aspect which is perhaps the most difficult and demands more patience: the religious and cultural aspect. It is not enough to have the Roman liturgy translated, celebrated in home-made garments and accompanied with local hymns and musical instruments, to consider the worship incarnated. The translation of the Bible and teaching of catechesis in local languages is indeed a great step. But it does not necessarily mean that the message of the gospel has been incarnated or inculturated. Incarnation or inculturation is not a skin-deep affair. It is more profound and more demanding. It requires digging deeper. This is why, unless the local religious tradition is taken seriously and the whole set-up of the local culture is duly considered and put in dialogue with the gospel, the church will never be incarnated, still less the message of her mission be inculturated.

In Mozambique there was some hope in this direction when, at the time of independence, the local priests, men and women religious had succeeded in forming a sort of religious association: USAREMO (Uniâo dos Sacerdotes e religiosos Moçambicanos). Its aim was very clear, at least for the members:

Safeguarding the plurality and the charism proper to each institute and without any interferences in the private life of the religious institutes, USAREMO has as its aim to unite, through meetings and other adequate means, all the Mozambiquan ecclesiastics, brothers and sisters . . . Each region will be entrusted with a task of study and research which will be put at the service of the episcopal conference and of the Mozambiquan church.[22]

9. Alas! Such a raising of consciousness was a threat for those who had been used to see submissive Mozambiquans. Using a familiar policy, some specialists in 'socio-ecclesial theology' (ideology?) appeared who labelled USAREMO racist, and accused it of being an eventual source of religious syncretism and of a lack of Christian universality.

As was to be expected from people who for years had suffered from cultural alienation and politico-religious colonization, the tactical attack did not meet with any strong resistance. The association gradually grew weaker and has now almost disappeared from the scene.

USAREMO, besides being a means of mutual support, was mainly a body for study and reflection on Mozambiquan realities. It was indeed a promising bridgehead for the inculturation of the message of the gospel in the country. In fact, as we have seen above, tasks had already been distributed according to region. To the northern region, for instance, was entrusted the study of 'African Anthropology and Mozambiquan Society'.[23] So some moves had somehow been initiated. But now the interest is left to individual 'amateurs'!

10. In a situation like this, what can be said about the actuality of the church in ex-Portuguese Africa? Something has already been said along these lines, especially in answer to the question whether or not the church was incarnated in these countries. Suffice it to say here that there is the good will to make the church in an African reality capable of responding to the profound aspirations of the citizens of the countries in question. No doubt there are still obstacles to the move. However, all the signs seem to indicate that people have decided to overcome them.

Let us hope that this good will is a sign of a loyal and persevering search, which should make the statement of the bishops of Mozambique in their report to the Sacred Congregation for the Evangelization of Peoples more in keeping with actual reality:

> We are very conscious of our pastoral duty of making this local church more African, without depriving her of being fully Christian and catholic.[24]

Notes

1. Archives of the Generalate of the Missionaries of Africa, Rome, p. 95, quoted by

Gripekoven, *Mozambique, une Eglise, Signe du Salut . . . Pour qui?*, 1973.

2. Henrique P. Rema, *História das Missôes Católicas da Guiné*, Braga 1982, 12.

3. A. da Silva Rego, *Liçôes de Missionologia*, Lisbon 1961, 273, 296.

4. Article 15 of the Missionary Agreement, 7 May 1940.

5. Article 7 of the Missionary Agreement, 7 May 1940.

6. Bull *Solemnibus conventionibus*, 1940.

7. Gripekoven, *Mozambique, une Eglise* (n. 1).

8. *Estatuto Missionário*, Decreto-lei 30207, 5 April 1941.

9. Quoted by Rema, *História das Missôes Católicas* (n. 2), 527.

10. Luis de Camoes, *The Lusiads*, First Song, v. 2.

11. Rema, *História das Missôes Católicas* (n. 2), 540.

12. Gripekoven, *Mozambique, une Eglise* (n. 1), 110f.

13. *Datas e Documentos da História da Frelimo*, Imprensa Nacional 1975, 495f.

14. Article 14 of the Constitution of the People's Republic of Mozambique.

15. *Carta Pastoral dos Bispos Católicos de Moçambique*, 25 April 1980, nos. 4–5.

16. *Assembleia Nacional de Pastoral*, Beira, September 1977, 1.

17. Ibid., nos. 2, 8.

18. *Testemunhar a Fé em Liberdade. Carta Pastoral dos Bispos Católicos de Moçambique*, 3 December 1978, no. 2.

19. Ibid.

20. *Assembleia Nacional de Pastoral* (n. 16), no. 20.

21. Cf. the pastoral letters of the episcopal conference.

22. *Estatutos da USAREMO*, 2 February 1975, nos. 2, 5.

23. Ibid.

24. *Relatório da Conferência Episcopal de Moçambique à Sagrada Congr. Evangelizacâo dos Povos*, 1982, II.3.

Being the Church in an Islamic Society

Henri Teissier

By definition, the African Synod involves the whole continent. This indicates the place that the relationship of the church to Islam should have in it. In fact, at least a third of the inhabitants of Africa are Muslims. Granted, the countries which are totally Muslim or at least have a very large Muslim majority are almost all situated in Arab Africa or in the region bordering on the Sahel. But other countries, on the Gulf of Guinea or in East Africa, also have Muslim populations equal or almost equal to the Christian population. For example, one might cite Nigeria, with 40% Muslims, amounting to at least 40 million people; Tanzania with 30%; the Ivory Coast with 25–30%; Cameroon with 15%; and Benin with 15%. In fact the majority of African countries have a Muslim population. The *Lineamenta* have taken account of this by introducing in chapter 3, on dialogue, a section which tackles the problem of the relations with Islam and with Muslims (nos. 62–68).

There can be no question here of analysing the content of the proposals which have been made in the *Lineamenta* on this theme. I would simply like to show how there is a way of being 'the church in an Islamic society', i.e. of having responsibility for the gospel and bearing witness to the gospel, in relations with Islam and with Muslims. One cannot say that all the Christian communities of the areas with a large Muslim presence have really asked themselves about their responsibility for evangelization in relation to Islam.[1] Many churches have too much on their hands, catechizing Christians who come from traditional African religion, and building up the structures needed for the life of a young Christian community and its inculturation, to find the time and the means for a real relationship with Islam and with Muslims. But we cannot leave out this aspect of the church's mission to Africa if we are to respond to the aims of the synod, 'The Church in Africa and its Mission of Evangelization'.

The synod must be an occasion for the churches of Africa to check how faithful they are to their mission, by reflecting together on the different aspects of their responsibility. So each particular church is invited to communicate its own experience to others. That is why this article will contain an account of the situation of the church in Algeria, from the particular perspective of its view of its relationship to Islam and to Muslims. One could have given a similar account of the other churches of the Maghreb, above those in Tunisia and Morocco, and also, to a lesser degree, in Mauritania or Libya. To keep things simple, I shall begin solely from the Algerian situation. However, the aim of this account will not be to describe the specific situation of Christians in Algeria but to investigate what it can be to 'act as the church' in an Islamic country, or, better still, what it can be to evangelize the relationship to Islam and to Muslims.

The very small Christian communities of Algeria in a Muslim society

The church in Algeria looks disconcerting to those who encounter it from outside.[2] Almost all the Christians are foreigners, coming from a great variety of countries: Western or Eastern Europe, the Middle East (above all Copts) and Black Africa (above all students). Together, all those baptized do not add up to more than 30,000 people in a country of 25 million, all Muslims.

And yet there is a 'church of Algeria'. In fact in Algeria those in transit find a nucleus of resident Christians who help them to share in being Christians of Algeria, however brief their stay in the country may be.

The permanent nucleus which thus gives the church its complexion and its vocation is also made up of several groups. First of all there are the 170 priests and male religious and the 400 women religious. This is a considerable number in proportion to the total number of Christians. But the priests and religious are not there to serve the Christians; they are there for Algeria, and to help the whole Christian community to understand itself and find a place as the 'church of Algeria', a Muslim country. In this effort they are helped by several hundred lay 'missionaries', i.e. people who have chosen to live in Algeria as their Christian vocation, although they would have the oppportunity to go elsewhere, and humanly speaking that would make life easier and professionally more secure for them.

To this group must be added the Christian wives of Algerian Muslims. There are several thousand of these, of very different nationalities. Since they are married to Algerians, their children are Algerian. Although they were born outside Algeria and maintain links with their country of birth, they are irrevocably tied to Algeria through their husbands and their children. Finally, there is also a small group of Algerian Christians, almost all descendants of families who came to know the gospel during the period of the French presence. They are in a difficult situation, given the Muslim character of the society. However, they have made the choice to stay in Algeria, to be the centre of this 'Christian church of Muslim Algeria'.

In the Middle East, Black Africa and Asia, there are many other Christians scattered in towns and societies which are entirely Muslim. The very character of our church of Algeria, which is its permanent nucleus and gives a direction to others, is the conception that it forms a church for the Muslim Algerian society. Priests, religious and lay 'missionaries' want to be Christians in the midst of Muslims and for Muslims. In other Muslim countries outside the Maghreb one can find some Christians who orientate their whole lives on an evangelical relationship to Islam.

What is truly peculiar to the church of Algeria and the other churches of the Maghreb is that the whole of the local church is called to a relationship to Islam. Imitating the vocabulary of the religious congregations, one could say that in a way the church of Algeria finds its basic charism and its *raison d'être* in this relation to Islam and to Muslims.

In Algeria, for more than a century, Christians have been learning to make a church 'for' Muslims

In the context which I have just described, how have the Christians formed their own idea of the mission of their church? For an answer, we have to make a historical detour.[3] In 1868 in Algiers, Cardinal Lavigerie founded the White Fathers and the White Sisters. He made it their mission to live among the Muslims, and to learn from them their language – Arabic, but also in some regions Berber – their customs and the values of Algerian and Muslim society. For more than a century these missionaries – priests, brothers or women religious – have lived like this among the Muslims, as though the Muslims were their parish, visiting families, founding schools or centres of professional training for them, and running youth groups, all Muslim. For example, in Kabylie in the 1940s the White Sisters founded a youth movement for the young local girls, who of course were Muslims. It was called 'The Beehive'. In it they presented to the young girls the best insights of the scout movement and Catholic Action, but without any explicit reference to the gospel. The White Fathers did the same thing in the Muslim scout troops that they looked after, in a kind of 'chaplaincy', and did all this while respecting the religious identity of the young Muslims. This led to a conviction in the church of Algeria, based on experience, that one could be a Christian and even a missionary and yet engage in activities of witness and service in an entirely Muslim milieu, for people who intended to remain Muslims.

Another source of the missionary experience of our church should be mentioned. That is the life of the Brothers of Charles de Foucauld, whose witness among the Muslim population of the Sahara, first at Beni Abbès, and then at Hoggar among the Tuaregs, was to serve as a basic model for two congregations of the Little Brothers and the Little Sisters of Jesus, both of which came into being in Algeria between 1930 and 1940. The disciples of Brother Charles were not concerned, as were the White Fathers, to establish ways of training or educating Muslims; they just lived as Christians among Muslims, very simply, because Jesus invites us to become 'little universal brothers'. This spiritual movement has inspired not only congregations which recognize the spirit of Fr de Foucauld as their basic charism, but also the whole of our church, and beyond that the universal church.[4]

These two missionary experiences, that of the White Fathers and White Sisters, and that of the Little Brothers and Little Sisters of Jesus, were enriched and extended during the Algerian war of liberation. Granted, the majority of Christians of European origin refused to understand the basic questions raised by the political and cultural claims of the national Algerian Muslim movement. However, following Cardinal Duval, Fr Jean Scotto who was to become Bishop of Constantine, Jesuit fathers, priests of the Mission de France, a group of brave laity and many others, along with religious from various congregations, laity from Catholic Action, from the scout movement, from Catholic Aid and so on, the church of Algeria learned to commit itself actively, in solidarity with the Algerians, for justice and respect for human rights in a very difficult situation. This was a situation of war, of violence, of torture and of confrontations between the European and Muslim populations. In this context a third source sprang up to shape the pastoral experience of the church of Algeria, that of shared commitment with Muslims for the defence of human rights.[5]

Finally, a fourth source was to give life to our 'church for Algeria' at the time of the country's independence in 1962. Within a few weeks, almost all the European Christians, who had been established in Algeria for a century or even longer, decided to leave the country, giving up life in a Muslim society. The permanent nucleus which I have mentioned was then left there alone. For all its members, Christian vocation took on a direction which one could sum up like this: to implement with our Muslim partners the will of God for us, Christians and Muslims, above all through enterprises of training and human development, but also quite simply in everyday life. Religious congregations which hitherto had worked in a European Christian milieu saw their schools, their dispensaries, their workrooms, their girls' hostels, their kindergartens, completely full of Muslim children, the young, or sick people. What had been above all the vocation of the White Fathers, the White Sisters, the spiritual family of Fr de Foucauld, and some militant Christians, from now on became the vocation of all, including parishes in which priests started remedial courses for young Muslims whose education had been set back by the war, or took a professional job in Muslim society.

From the colonial church in which only some Christians recognized a vocation to live out an evangelical relationship with the Muslims, there grew up a new way of life, shared by the whole local church, that of becoming in some way a church for Algeria, although the society is Muslim and *a priori* has provided no place for Christians as such. Christians sought to be the church in a Muslim society.

A church with a relationship to Islam and to the Muslims which has deepened its vocation since Vatican II

The church of Algeria, and more widely that of North Africa, had its place in the reflections of the universal church which, at Vatican II, sought the *aggiornamento* of its vocation and mission in relation to believers of other religions. Several experts who played a part in the preparation of the decree *Nostra Aetate* had had experience of a relationship with Islam and with Muslims while they were in Algeria or Tunisia. These people were to continue to be involved in the first stages of the work of the Roman Secretariat for Non-Christians, giving this new structure the perspective for its work and its first orientation, within the framework of the renewal of the theology of the church which the Council had achieved. One thinks in particular of Louis Gardet (a Little Brother from Algeria), Fr Cuocq (the first secretary, for Islam, of the Roman Secretariat for Non-Christians), of Frs Lanfry, Caspar, Abd el Jallil, Anawati, Borrmans, etc. (all consultants to the new Secretariat), who began their life with Muslims in North Africa, even if Fr Anawati came from a Middle Eastern country (Egypt).[6]

Our vocation as a 'church for the Muslims' was born spontaneously out of the pastoral experience of the church of Algeria and, beyond that, of the church of North Africa. But Vatican II gave each of us all the points of reference necessary for understanding this mission. To demonstrate that, we need only take the encyclical which Pope John Paul II has just issued on mission, *Redemptoris Missio*. Vatican II is the theological basis of his reflections. But the consequences of the intuitions of the Council have been broadened and deepened by the experience of dialogue with non-Christians which the church has had since the Council. Chapter 3 of this document, entitled 'The Holy Spirit – The Principal Agent of Mission', illustrates very clearly how the church's conception of its mission has been enriched. As no. 28 of this document states: 'The Spirit's presence and activity are universal, limited neither by space nor time. No man can respond to its highest calling' without the 'light and strength of the Spirit'. Quoting *Dominum et vivificantem*, the Pope adds: 'The Spirit is at the very source of man's existential and religious questioning, a questioning which is occasioned not only by contingent situations but by the very structure of his being' (DV 54 and RM 28).

According to Vatican II, the church from now on has the conviction that at the heart of all human existence the response given by each person has a place between the call of the Spirit, the freedom of the individual, the events of his or her life, and the conditions of his or her own culture. It is from this culture that individuals derive their religion, but it is only in the Spirit that they can understand their true vocation and respond to it. This theological certainty gives a new dimension to the mission of the church and the Christian. It helps us to understand that there is a living element in every person which enables all to respond faithfully to the call of the Spirit in them. This shared work, aimed at liberating within us the energies of the Holy Spirit, brings in the kingdom of God. It constitutes the vast people of God, whose face we see in the face of Christ and in the life of the church, but which in every respect surpasses the church already gathered. Referring to the inter-religious experience and encounter at Assisi, and the reflection which it prompted, the Pope sees this action of the Spirit in the prayer of every believer, regardless of his or her religion; 'Every authentic prayer is prompted by the Holy Spirit, who is mysteriously present in every human heart' (RM 29).

The Pope also affirms what he has just said about the personal experience of every human being in connection with their collective experience: 'The Spirit's presence and activity affect not only individuals but also society and history, peoples, cultures and religions. Indeed, the Spirit is at the origin of the noble ideals and undertakings which benefit humanity on its journey' (RM 28). We can see the importance of these words for establishing a new Christian attitude to other religions. In the collective religious heritage of a given human community, one has to recognize, welcome and stimulate all that comes from the Holy Spirit.[7]

These few reflections might seem to be taking us away from the theme of the African Synod. However, in fact they shed light on the plans and aims for the synod in its relationship to Islam and to Muslims.

Let us return to Algeria. Those who take a quick look at our communities are sometimes led to express their views on what we are in dismissive comments like, 'Basically you're simply social.' Or, 'This is simply a silent presence in the midst of Muslims.' Such a way of looking at things is quite inadequate. Ours is not a 'silent' witness. All our Muslim partners know that we are Christians. They see us praying in our chapels. They see the springs of our religious life in our ties to the church, to Jesus and his gospel. They soon discover that service of the neighbour is the touchstone of our faithfulness. They are amazed and disconcerted at the commitment to celibacy dedicated to God, and aimed at achieving the availability which priests and religious want to offer to God and their fellow human beings. Muslims also see the lives of Christian married couples characterized in freedom, in responsibility between the partners and the relationship of trust which they have with their children. As long as the relations with Muslims last, they ask us questions about Christian customs of prayer and fasting, and even about the dogmas which mark the way in which we differ from their Islam. Often, moreover, it is not these questions which lead to the deepest sharing, but questions which arise out of events in life: suffering, conjugal fidelity, professional conscience, the religious law and freedom in the Spirit, and so on.

Thanks to this life together which comes from living in the same area or working in the same professional body, an exchange is coming about between specifically Christian values and those to which the Spirit of God gives birth in the life of members of the Muslim community, or which they inherit from their tradition. As John Paul II has said in *Redemptoris Missio*, this communication between individuals and communities in the name of God is part of the mission of the church: 'Inter-religious dialogue is part of the evangelizing mission of the church . . . This dialogue is based on hope and love, and it will bear fruit in the Spirit. Other religions constitute a positive challenge for the Church; they stimulate her both to discover and acknowledge the signs of Christ's presence and of the working of the Spirit, as well as to examine more deeply her own identity and to bear witness to fullness the Revelation which she has received for the good of all' (RM 56).[8]

A local church under the impact of Islam

However, to evangelize the relationship to Islam and the Muslims is not only to provide a concrete possibility for Muslims to get to know Christians and, through them, the church, the gospel and Christ. It is also to be on the receiving end, in the name of the universal church, of the questions posed to us by Islam. Certainly at the beginning of mission in Algeria there was a feeling of superiority which led 'missionaries' to be almost exclusively preoccupied with what they could bring to their Muslim partners in the name of Christ and within the framework of Christian certainties about morality, prayer, God, man, etc.

Things changed with the end of the colonial relationship. Church documents have demonstrated this change: *Ecclesiam suam*, Vatican II and all the reflections on dialogue within the framework of the Pontifical

Council for Inter-Religious relations, and in many statements by the Pope during his encounters with Muslims (Casablanca, 19 August 1985).[9] The conviction has grown that the evangelical relationship to the other must necessarily be established in two directions. Islam exists, and so do the Muslims. They have experience of the quest for God, of life in the universal and local community of believers. They have their way of praying, of fasting, of moral fidelity, of sharing with the poor, of mutual reconciliation, of hospitality. They discuss together, as they are doing at present with great vigour, how to implement the law of God, in the lives not only of individuals but also of societies.[10] They are asking questions about the aims they should set before their people, and about the kind of education and culture that will help believers to cope with modernity. And there are a billion people to whom to present these questions almost at the same time, even if the development of each Muslim society has its own rhythms.

Within Algeria, as Christians, we are not just spectators, but are actually taking part, through our friendships, in this spiritual history and this quest with planetary dimensions – occupying the difficult, but specific, place of the minority. We are putting all this human and spiritual history before God in our prayer and our eucharist. It takes hold of our whole being and penetrates our personal life, and it also pervades our mutual encounters, our plans for the future, our prayer and our reading of the Bible. Our future as a church does not depend primarily on us, but also on the direction taken by the Muslim community, and the place occupied in it by fundamentalist currents, charismatic leaders or personalities courageously engaged in reconciling modernity with fidelity to their Islam. The impact of Islam is also part of our mission. God has plans for these individuals and this religious community. Its destiny, in both its negative and its positive aspects, is part of the history of the people of God and relates to the coming of the kingdom. How we understand this adventure as Christians and explain it to the universal church is also the work of the gospel. For this is a history of human discussions with God here and now.

Evangelizing the relationship with Islam

It would have been possible to tackle our theme in many ways. I have not mentioned many questions which are important for the life of a church in an Islamic society. How does one secure respect for individual freedom of conscience in Islamic society? How does one reconcile the Muslim law with the life of non-Muslims in society? How does one raise questions about reciprocal relations between Christian and Muslim minorities or majorities? What progress can we expect from dialogue on doctrine between

Christian theologians and Muslim scholars (*ulamas* or *fuqaha*)?[11] What possibilities are there of a beginning of real sharing between Christians and Muslims in prayer?

Describing Islamic-Christian relations in Muslim Algeria could not provide answers to all these questions in the context of this prelude to the issues faced by the African Synod. One's only wish in giving the testimony of a 'church of Algeria for Muslim society' is to raise for the other local churches of Africa the question of the evangelization of their relationship to Islam and to the Muslims. We do not claim in any way to have found the true answer to this question, either for ourselves or for others. But we would like to bear witness that for us, this question is essential. We would like to explain that we are raising it in the hope that other local churches can profit from the preparation of the African Synod to raise it as well. What riches would come to the whole church in Africa if in this way we could share our experiences in the principal spheres of our responsibilities! That of relations with Islam is only one of them. The same sharing could also begin in other quite essential areas, like creating a church 'for justice and peace' or even a church which has left its Western and European strait-jacket to flourish in the cultures of Africa.

Translated by John Bowden

Notes

1. The Episcopal Commission on Relations between Christians and Muslims in West Africa regularly expresses this concern. It has published two documents aimed at mutual understanding: *Connais-tu ton frère?*, which presents Islam to Christians, and *Frères dans la foi au Dieu Unique* (both 1988), to explain Christianity to Muslims.

2. Three works may help towards a deeper knowledge of the particular witness of the church in Algeria in its relations with Islam and Muslims: *Le Cardinal Duval, évêque en Algérie*, conversations with Marie Christine Ray, Paris 1984; Henri Teissier, *Église en Islam*, Paris 1984; Jean Scotto, *Curé pied-noir et évêque algérien*, Paris 1991.

3. There is an overall account of the history of the church in Algeria and North Africa, with chapters on the missionary significance of the foundation of the White Fathers and White Sisters, and the spiritual families of Fr de Foucauld, in the collection of studies on the church of North Africa, *De St Augustin au Cardinal Duval, chrétiens d'Afrique du Nord du 2ᵉ siècle à nos jours*, Paris 1991.

4. Ibid., ch. 11.

5. On this cf. André Nozière, *Les Chrétiens pendant la guerre*, Paris 1979.

6. On this cf. Henri Teissier, 'L'expérience missionnaire de l'Eglise au Maghreb et la mission du Conseil Pontifical pour le dialogue inter-religieux', *Bulletin du Conseil Pontifical pour le dialogue inter-religieux* 72, 1989, 323–33.

7. This understanding of the relationship between Christians and non-Christians was already proposed by the episcopal conference of North Africa in its document *Le sens de nos rencontres, Documentation Catholique*, 2 December 1979, no. 21, p. 1032.

8. For this link between the various forms of mission and dialogue see my *La Mission de l'Eglise*, and also the account of the Francheville colloquium on mission, *Spiritus*, 1983, no. 94.

9. Cf. the text in *Documentation Catholique*, 6 October 1985, no. 17, p. 942.

10. As examples I simply quote a few works which reflect this debate: Ahmed Rouadjia, *Les frères et la mosquée*, Karthala 1990; Muhammad Said Al Ashmawy, *L'islamisme contre l'Islam*, Paris 1989; Daryush Shayegan, *Le regard mutilé*, Paris 1988; Mustapha Cherif, *L'islam a l'épreuve du temps*, Paris 1991.

11. There is an approach to the main questions raised here in *La foi en marche. Les problèmes de fond du dialogue islamo-chrétien*, Rome 1990, first published in Spanish: *Fe adelante*, Madrid 1988.

Being Church in an Islamo-Christian Society: Emerging Patterns of Christian/Muslim Relations in Africa – A Nigerian Perspective

John Olorunfemi Onaiyekan

Introduction

In November 1989, an epoch-making international conference was held in Abuja, Nigeria's new federal capital, on 'Islam in Africa'. It was organized by the major world Islamic movements, led by the Nigerian Supreme Council for Islamic Affairs, the Islamic Council in London and the Organization of Islamic Conferences (OIC). It was the first of its kind. Among its lofty objectives was 'to focus the attention of the Muslim world on the enormous potential of Islam in Africa'.[1] After the conference, judged by all participants as being very successful, a permanent body called 'Islam in Africa Conference' was established to explore and exploit the 'enormous potential of Islam in Africa' which the gathering had identified.

At the end of the historical introduction to the *Lineamenta* (outline) for the forthcoming Special Assembly for Africa of the Synod of Bishops, we read:

> An 'hour of Africa' appears to have come, a favourable 'hour' which calls on Christ's messengers to launch out into the deep in order to win Africa for Christ.[2]

Meanwhile, on a world level, the World Council of Churches had launched a 'Decade of Evangelization' 1991–2000, while in Catholic circles the 'Evangelization 2000' movement has set itself the target of presenting to

Christ a bimillennial birthday gift of 'a world more Christian than not'. The Christian churches in Africa are deeply and enthusiastically involved in these world movements.

It seems that this last decade of the second millennium is going to be very exciting indeed. In what is certainly a diplomatic understatement, the *Lineamenta* warns:

> As both Christians and Muslims seek to make many converts, great prudence will be required to avoid a dangerous collision course between Islam's *Da'wah* ('the Call') and Christian evangelization.[3]

There is no continent in which this 'collision course' is more obvious than in Africa. The question of Christian-Muslim relations has therefore become a major issue on our problem-infested continent.

This short reflection aims to show that Africa needs to go beyond the traditional patterns of Muslim-Christian relations if religious peace and harmony is to be maintained on the continent. The Nigerian case will be presented as an important illustration of the general African situation. I shall conclude with a suggestion that the rest of the world may have lessons to learn from the African experience.

1. Traditional patterns

For a long time, the classical patterns of Christian-Muslim relations were based on the assumption that a nation or people had to have its own religion. But since both Christianity and Islam each claimed to be a universal religion, rough encounters and rivalries became inevitable as each tried to 'win the whole world' to its faith. The result of the ensuing inconclusive battle is an uneasy truce by which many parts of the world become considered as Christian lands or Muslim nations.

In Christian lands, society was expected to be run along Christian principles. Historically and culturally, a Christian identity of some sort characterizes the people. Muslims are few. They live among Christians as visitors or immigrants. If they are conveniently ignored, they do not seem to expect anything more.

Nowadays, not many countries officially call themselves 'Christian'. But there are many nations in which the cultural and historical roots of their Christian past still run deep. In any case, many Muslims still tend to refer to countries of Europe and America as 'the Christian West'.

In Muslim lands, the sense of being an Islamic nation is very strong. Many such nations are officially called 'Islamic', e.g. Libya, Mauritania, Pakistan, etc. Here society is expected to be run along Islamic lines and much is made of the 'Sharia' or Islamic law. Christians may be few or quite a strong minority: they are at best tolerated. Often, they have to live under outright suppression. They are considered as second-class citizens who cannot claim equal personal and communal rights to Muslims. For their part, Christians, generally by historical tradition, accept the role and status allowed them.

Much of the thinking on Christian-Muslim relations, whether in Christian or Muslim circles, has arisen within the contexts described above. In Africa, some nations claim to be Muslim or Christian – or are aspiring to be such. They seek inspiration from countries they consider to be models of a good Christian or Islamic state. But on the whole, in Africa, the reality on the ground renders such 'models' inapplicable. What is this reality?

2. Christians and Muslims in Africa

Looking at Africa in general, I want to draw attention to a few general observations relevant to our discussion.

(i) Acquired religions

In Africa, both Christianity and Islam are acquired religions. If Christianity is often dismissed as a religion 'foreign' to Africa, it must also be acknowledged that Islam did not originate from our continent. From that point of view, both are strangers.

But then, for every continent, both Christianity and Islam are historical religions, each with a relatively recent historical point of departure in the context of world history. The older of the two, Christianity, is only 2000 years old; Islam is 600 years younger still. Thus, wherever these religions exist today, they have been recently acquired. Every Christian nation *became* Christian within the last 2000 years; all Muslim lands *became* Muslim within the last 1400 years. From this point of view, all nations are in the same basic condition of 'converts' to whichever of the two religions they claim as their own.

Furthermore, we need to remind ourselves that the continent of Africa was present at the origins of both religions. The child Jesus spent some time with the Holy Family in Egypt (Matt. 2.13–23); Africans were in Jerusalem on the day of Pentecost (Acts 2.8–12). When there was already a flourishing church in Alexandria (Egypt) and Carthage (Tunisia), much of present-day Europe was still pagan. Islam, too, spread to Africa within its first generation, again through Egypt. It is also significant that the 'Muslim lands' of Africa today are built on the ruins of an early Christianity which lasted many centuries, not only in Egypt, Tunis, Libya, Algeria and the Magherib lands in general, but also further south in the Sudan and Somalia where the Nubian church survived for about a thousand years *after* Islam.[4] Christian-Muslim relations in Africa have a long history, with many phases and diverse faces.

(ii) Shared experiences

Africa has opened up to both Islam and Christianity in such a way that in many countries, Christians and Muslims find themselves living side by side, sharing common experiences of life. In most nations, they share the same traditional *culture*, and are challenged to cope with reconciling this common cultural root with the new religions they have embraced. They face the same socio-political and economic predicament and the heavy task of contributing towards building modern nations within the present-day world context. Thus, the Christian or Muslim in Africa does not define his identity only in terms of religious affiliation, but also in terms of other important factors like nationality, tribe and social class. This often affects Christian-Muslim relations in a positive manner, as we are forced to work together on our common interests. Even if we quarrel every now and then, we remain brothers and sisters all the same, not strangers to one another.

(iii) A common home

Thus, in most of Africa, Christians and Muslims consider their nations a common home for everyone where everyone should feel, and be made to feel, equally at home. We expect more than mere tolerance of each other. We insist on mutual recognition and respect, as a basis for mutual collaboration in building nations that are united in their diversities.

(iv) Centrifugal forces

At the same time, there are forces tending to split our communities along Christian-Muslim lines, often with disastrous consequences to the peace and stability of our nations.

On the internal level within nations, where other centrifugal forces like tribal identity and political affiliation are reinforced by Christian-Muslim rivalries, national cohesion is put under severe strain. The Sudan is a case in point. On the international level, the influence of foreign centres of fanaticism and religious integralism create serious problems for our relations at home. Both among Christians and Muslims, there are fanatics who are tempted to aspire to making their nations such that their religion is not only dominant, but dominating. Thus, foreign models are evoked which have no possibility of a peaceful and just realization. Islam seems more particularly prone to this temptation, as the call for the Islamic state rings out from different parts of Africa, e.g. Nigeria, Senegal, etc.

(v) An ongoing struggle

Perhaps all this can be seen as part of the growing pains of African nations, most of which achieved political independence within the last thirty years. We are now at a critical stage in the political development of our nations. The decade ahead promises to be not only exciting, but decisive. Meanwhile, the struggle continues. Let us see the main outlines of this struggle in the case of Nigeria, Africa's greatest nation, with special focus on Christian-Muslim relations.

3. The Nigerian case

Nigeria, with its over one hundred million inhabitants, is the greatest African nation in many respects. It was Archbishop Teissier of Algiers who after a brief visit to Nigeria described it as 'the greatest Islamo-Christian nation in the world'. By this, he means that there is no nation in the world where there are so many Christians living side by side with so many Muslims. This in itself makes Nigeria an important test-case for evolving new patterns of Muslim-Christian relations in Africa and in the world at large.

(i) The traditional religions

Every discussion on religions in Nigeria – and indeed in Africa in general – should begin with the religion of the traditional cultures. In general, every ethnic group had its own religion and acknowledged that others had theirs. There was no 'missionary thrust' to convert others. This has in many cases formed a good cultural basis for the acknowledgement of religious pluralism. On the other hand, each ethnic community lived in an integrated society in which politics, religion and social life in general formed one unit. This creates problems for the modern society of 'one nation, many religions', and affects Christian-Muslim relations in many ways.

In respect of the ethnic diversities in our nation, Christianity and Islam, each in its own way, have served as a unifying factor, as they draw their adherents from the different tribes, who then find themselves 'brothers' in the same faith. At the same time, the divergent approaches to the traditional religions can at times raise problems for Christian-Muslim relations.

(ii) Islam

Historically, Islam arrived in Nigeria before Christianity. There is evidence of Islamic presence in the Bornu area of Nigeria as early as around AD 1000, less than 400 years after Muhammad. From then until now,

Islam has spread to the north and west of Nigeria largely by peaceful infiltration, especially through the ruling classes. For a long time, it would seem that in Nigeria we had an easy-going type of Islam which lived in peace with the traditional religions, and left intact the traditional political system of the different tribes. The Jihad led by Othman dan Fodio which swept most of Northern Nigeria around 1830 undertook a drastic 'purification' of the previously existing Islam. From this religious, social and political movement emerged what has now come to be called the 'Sokoto caliphate', whose influence is still strongly felt today in the northern emirates.

Yorubaland in the south has also strong Muslim influence, but here Islam has remained integrated within the Yoruba traditional society which embraces both Christians and Muslims on an equal basis.

(iii) Christianity

Christianity made its first contact with present-day Nigeria through the Portuguese who visited Warri and Benin from Sao Tome from around 1550. By 1600, we hear of a devout Catholic king of Warri called Sebastian. But this enterprise was heavily dependent on the Portuguese, whose historical vicissitudes it shared. By 1800, there was little left to show for it. However, by then, a new wave of Christian missionary activity had started through both Protestant and Catholic missionaries. It is this new wave which has flowered into the present Christian presence in Nigeria.

Thus, Christianity spread to the north from the south: slowly at first, and later more rapidly, especially during the British colonial era and afterwards. We should not forget, however, that between 1700 and 1720 an attempt had been made to establish a Catholic presence in the Bornu kingdom by Franciscans operating from Tripoli across the desert. That the enterprise failed does not detract from its significance: Christianity, too, can move across the desert. This, by the way, challenges the Nigerian church to look northwards as it develops a missionary programme of its own.

(iv) British colonialism

British colonialism in Nigeria effectively started in the year 1900. By that time, Christian missions had made good progress in the south of Nigeria. This disproves the general assumption that Christianity came into Nigeria through colonialism.

By 1900, there was a strong Muslim presence in the north, a pretty extensive Christian presence and Christian missionary outreach in and from the south, and a large 'middle belt' uncommitted to either Christianity or Islam. British colonialism had its own specific objectives which hardly included Christianization. Indeed, when the activities of Christian missionaries went against British colonial interests, the latter prevailed. If

Christianity and Islam were rivals during the colonial era, we now see the role of Britain as one of a *partial* umpire, with sympathies for the northern Islamic establishment. Effectively, the British ruled Nigeria as two distinct entities, a Muslim north and non-Muslim south. We are still reaping today the legacy of this 'divide and rule' strategy. We have inherited a country that is divided and almost ungovernable! If there were not many clashes between Christians and Muslims in the colonial era, it was largely because the British kept both groups very much apart.

Post-independence integration

Nigeria gained political independence in 1960. Since then, it has been engaged in the tedious task of building a united nation. This process has led to many crises. Traditional political institutions have had to adjust to the all-embracing power of the national government. Thus, we have the irony of local tribal rulers enjoying more power and prestige under the colonial regime than in an independent Nigeria. This has affected the status of the Muslim rulers in the north, a situation that they find difficult to understand or accept.

Meanwhile, communications have improved, permitting Nigerians to move around, and breaking down many previous social barriers. This has made social interaction between Christians and Muslims inevitable, and intensified the task of finding the route to peaceful co-existence.

The civil war of 1967–70, often called the 'Biafran war', was fought 'to keep Nigeria one'. It, too, has brought north and south together. Both civilian and military régimes remind the nation that the price we paid for our *national* unity is high.

(vi) Growing pains

It is against this process of national integration that one should assess the periodic religious clashes and crises which Nigeria has been witnessing in recent years. The big question is whether we can live and grow together as one nation, and if so, what type of nation. Many Muslims who are agitating for an Islamic state in Nigeria tend to look back with nostalgia at the Sokoto caliphate; or outside with admiration at the 'model' Islamic states of the Arab world. But Nigeria is neither of these. The value of the crises, bloody though they may at times be, is gradually to clarify the situation – until we all agree to live in peace.

At present, a heated debate is raging on the secular nature of the Nigerian state. It is more than a disagreement on the meaning of words. It has to do with agreeing on what place religion should have in the nation. So far, there is a general agreement, and an official government stand on two points:

(a) That Nigeria shall not be a godless nation.
(b) That there shall be no official state religion in Nigeria.

Between these two extremes, a lot of issues still remain to be resolved, most of them carried over from our past history. Such issues include the place of the Sharia' in the legal system of the country; the role of the Muslim emirs as religious leaders as well as 'traditional rulers'; the rumour of Nigeria's membership of the Organization of Islamic Conferences (OIC), a rumour that has been neither confirmed nor denied officially by our government, etc.

Despite everything, there is a *de jure* equality of all religions in the country. Every citizen has the right to protest if he is in any way victimized on the basis of religion. *De facto*, however, injustice exists – not only on a religious basis, but on tribal, social, political and other lines. The ambition that Nigerians are nursing is to show the world that it is possible for Christians and Muslims to live together in equality, peaceful co-existence and mutual respect.

Conclusion

I believe that the struggles of Nigeria for an Islamo-Christian society have relevance not only for other African countries, but for the world at large, Christianity and Islam are the world's two greatest religions. That fact alone has made Christian-Muslim relations a world issue.

The classical patterns of relationship based on 'minority concessions' are no longer adequate to cope with the emerging realities in our world of today. There are no more isolated Christian lands and Muslim nations. The whole planet earth is becoming one big world community. The Gulf War has shown that whatever happens in one section of the world concerns every other part. That the line of battle during that war cut across Christian-Muslim boundaries goes to stress this point.

In the traditional Christian lands, Muslims are no longer just occasional visitors and migrants. In many places, they have become a strong and growing minority whose religious needs have to be catered for. On the whole, with the general trend of secularization and the strong concern for minority rights, Muslims in Christian lands have been enjoying a good deal of freedom and attention. At times, it appears to some of us that too much is being done – as governments and even churches practically undertake the promotion of Islam (e.g. donating churches to Muslims for prayers!). But recently some notes of alarm have been sounded in some countries where growing Muslim influence is being gradually perceived as a threat to national identity and culture. A new pattern of relationship, therefore, is called for.

In traditional Muslim lands, there is a long history of links with Christianity. Almost all of them were lands previously under Christian influence before Islam arrived. The memories of the historical experience of the Crusades linger on and easily float to the surface. Most of these lands have also gone through the domination of Western colonialism – which they also call 'Christian' colonialism. Today, there is the economic and technological impact of the West, which is making inevitable inroads into the Islamic society. Despite fundamentalist eruptions here and there, Islam cannot postpone indefinitely its appointment with modernity. The many social upheavals and political ferments within the Muslim world call for a reappraisal of traditional systems of living and patterns of relationship. The long denial of the rights of Christians to exercise their religion freely in Muslim lands will become less and less tolerable. The pope's recent remarks on this issue, quoted in the *Lineamenta*, are clear and timely.[5]

Finally, the more Islam succeeds in its aspirations of being a world religion, the more its Arabic texture is challenged. Already, there are far more Muslims outside Arab lands than inside. There are more Muslims in Nigeria than in Saudi Arabia, Iraq and Kuwait put together. The nation with the greatest number of Muslims is Indonesia. Many Muslims in non-Arab lands are asserting their cultural identity, insisting on a distinction between Islamic faith and Arabic culture in a new and vigorous way. This trend will have far-reaching effects on Christian-Muslim relations worldwide. Here, too, we must locate the significant role of Christian Arabs living in Arab lands in the formulation of a more just pattern of Christian-Muslim relations.

Christianity as a religion draws its inspiration from Jesus Christ, the Prince of Peace. Islam, we are told, stands for peace. If the two religions are to contribute effectively to peace in the world, they must find ways of living with one another in peace and mutual respect.

Notes

1. 'A Celebration of Unity', *Africa Events* 6.2, February 1990, 23–6.
2. Synod of Bishops, *Lineamenta for the Special Assembly for Africa*, no. 13.
3. *Lineamenta*, no. 65.
4. On the Nubian church, see J. A. Ilovbare, 'Christianity in Nubia', *Tarikh* 2.1, 53–61.
5. John Paul II, 'Address to the Diplomatic Corps' (13 January 1990), *L'Osservatore Romano* (weekly edition in English), 29 January 1990, 3. See also the good quotation in *Lineamenta*, no. 66.

Being a Christian in South Africa

Simon S. Maimela

I. Introduction

In normal circumstances, and especially in a country which prides itself as being 75% Christian, perhaps nothing could have been easier than to be asked to write a paper in which I should discuss what it is like to be a Christian in a Christian country. In other words, if I were to discuss the assigned topic in general terms, my task would be easy because one could, with justification, limit the description of what it means to be a Christian to activities in which people are involved in the life of the church. Alternatively, one might limit the discussion to the verbal profession of Christians, such as, for instance, their affirmation that they are saved from sin and death through God's grace alone; that they are brothers and sisters in Christ by reason of their one baptism, one faith and one Lord; and therefore that they must care, serve and love one another as God has loved first.

However appealing this general way of talking about being Christian in South Africa may be, it has to be conceded that this way of talking hides more than it reveals about the state of Christian presence in that part of the world. For in real life, and particularly in South Africa, men and women are not simply Christians in general who as such are members of human society in general. Rather, the fact of the matter is that real Christians, like the rest of people living in South Africa, always exist concretely in particular communities in which white Christians hold certain positions and are accorded certain privileges and rights, while black Christians are denied possibilities for personal growth and self-realization. In consequence, we do not have just one but different types of being Christian in South Africa. Therefore, with justification the *Kairos Document* laments the fact that the church is divided between white and black Christians.[1]

On the one hand, there are white Christians who, as conquerors and the dominant group, are rich. On the other, there are also the dominated and oppressed black Christians who are denied social, political and economic rights. This situation reflects the history of South Africa, which has been one of continuous struggle and strife between whites and blacks over the land, over gold and other material resources, since white colonialists set foot on this country. After the subjugation of the black majority, white Christians have used religion to give moral justification for material and other economic self-interests at the expense of blacks. Reflecting on and being conditioned by the world of white Christian colonizers, Christian theology became unabashedly racist in its justification of the so-called rights of white people. Even at present, these rights of white people (sometimes euphemistically referred to as minority rights) are still being defended by the reformist government of President de Klerk, who is supposedly working for a new South Africa.

This theology of oppression (as opposed to the theology of liberation), which gives religious sanction to white privilege to a point of dividing the Christians into two groups, could rightly be called 'white colonial theology'. Its most distinguishing feature lies in its teaching of an authoritarian God, who, as the Supreme Being in the universe, establishes racial classes in every society. Hence this God insists that there will always be the rich and poor in every society, because this God accepts poverty as part of the divine will for the underdogs, while wealth is given to the mighty and powerful in society, who happen to be whites in South Africa. To ensure that this situation of unequal distribution of material resources remains unchanged, 'white colonial theology' teaches that God has established law and order in every society and, above all, demands obedience to the authority of both the state and church.[2] This misuse of religion to justify socio-political and economic interests is best articulated by Napoleon, who, long before Karl Marx published his *Communist Manifesto* (1848), has this to say concerning colonial theology:

> As far as I am concerned, I do not see in religion the mystery of the incarnation but the mystery of social order: it links the idea of inequality to heaven which prevents the rich person from being murdered by the poor . . . How can there be order in the state without religion? Society cannot exist without inequality of fortunes and the inequality of fortunes could not subsist without religion. Whenever a half-starved person is near another who is glutted, it is impossible to reconcile the difference if there is not an authority to say to him: 'God wills it so, it is necessary that there be rich and poor in the world, but afterwards in eternity there will be a different distribution.'[3]

II. The Black Experience

In the light of the fact that Christians as well as church life are divided along racial lines, my discussion of being a Christian in South Africa will largely be influenced by my black experience under white domination, commonly known as *Apartheid*.[4] This political system cruelly places a heavy weighty significance on the fact that a person is born either white or black. For it is on the basis of one's colour of skin that a person is declared by law justified or unjustified to enjoy certain economic, political and cultural rights and privileges. Since it is the black people who have borne the brunt of *Apartheid*, this political system symbolizes the negation of the people of colour, a negation of their humanity, dignity, security and justice. For *Apartheid* was designed and practised in such a way that blacks would be continually reminded that they are *unworthy persons*, regardless of whether they were Christians or not. At the same time, the *Apartheid* system taught whites, regardless of whether they are Christians or not, that they deserve a particular life-style and enormous political and economic privileges which are due to them by some natural right: that is, by virtue of their right colour. Put somewhat differently, we have in *Apartheid* human attempts to theologize politics and thereby transform politics into an instrument of self-justification, self-salvation, and self-preservation. For through this political system the white minority government has promised to save whites both in body and soul, provided they vote for it, while the black non-voters are condemned to a sub-human existence of oppression and domination.

III. Seeking to be Christian in an unjust racial society

The ideology of *Apartheid* poses a serious challenge to both white and black Christians, because its fundamentally teaching and practice contradict the central message of the Christian faith, namely, that life is a divine gift and also that sinful humanity is saved solely through God's grace and mercy.[5] Over against this fundamental Christian teaching, *Apartheid*, through its promotion of white self-salvation and self-preservation, has encouraged whites to take their lives and future into their own hands. That is, *Apartheid* has taught whites to believe that they can save themselves in the face of dangers that the black majority posed for them, and thus gives whites life rather than their receiving it from God, the Creator. Therefore, trying to be Christians in a racial South Africa, whites are challenged to reject the *Apartheid* ideology which has set itself as an idol that promises to save white people both in soul and body. For to embrace *Apartheid* would be an expression of lack of faith in God the Creator and Saviour, in whose hands human life (including that of white people) ought to be placed. Indeed, because whites have struggled for so long to survive in a hostile African environment, what they need most is not the law of self-salvation and self-preservation, but the real life-giving message of the gospel which proclaims to them that life is a free gift from God, who in Christ has also procured salvation for humanity. *Apartheid* also poses a serious challenge to blacks who are seeking to be Christians. For, as we have indicated above, *Apartheid* does not make God's relation to humans the criterion for human dignity and integrity, but the genetic and factors of race which distinguish between superior and inferior races. The consequence of this for black people has been devastating, by making them feel inferior and inadequate, leading to such attempts as trying to use lightening creams to change their black skins or treatment for their short curly hair. Condemning the negative effects of the *Apartheid* system on blacks, Archbishop Desmond Tutu, with deep insight, writes:

> *Apartheid* is intrinsically and irredeemably evil. For my part, its most vicious, indeed its most blasphemous aspect, is not the great suffering it causes its victims, but that it can make a child of God doubt that he is a child of God. For that alone, it deserves to be condemned as a heresy. Real peace and security will come to our beloved land only when *Apartheid* has been dismantled.[6]

As opposed to what *Apartheid* teaches, black Christians have an important role in this situation in reminding white Christians that all human beings are unworthy, unacceptable and sinners before the righteous God, and therefore that no race or group is any better than another. For God in Christ accepts (justifies) sinful people not on account of their merits (racial worthiness) but solely out of sheer divine grace and steadfast love.

IV. The unmasking and relativization of Apartheid as an idol

Given the fact that *Apartheid* has tried to indoctrinate and lead people to believe that human identity is to be found primarily in one's racial group, those who are seeking to be Christians in South Africa are challenged to become aware that racialism is a theological problem which must be unmasked as an idol and relativized. Without denying the beauty and richness of humankind which expresses itself through the diversity of different colours, ethnic and cultural manifestations, Christians in South Africa are challenged to struggle against the mistaken tendency of allowing race to be venerated as an absolute, an idol or god which seeks to enslave its worshippers, thus tempting them into the sin of self-idolization. Indeed, Christians must challenge South Africans to become aware that racism has become what Kosuke Koyama once referred to as 'pornographic', namely, that racism has 'exalted a particular biological attribute (other than sexual) out of all proportion and removed it from a context where it was properly significant'.[7] Rather than becoming engrossed and participating in the pornographic nature of racism, Christians have the task of reminding South Africans that Christian living involves the daily dying and putting away of the 'old Adam' so that it may be replaced by the 'new Adam'.

Furthermore, Christians should remind South Africans that a genuine identity is not given by the idolatrous god of race, but is found and given to us in Jesus Christ, who alone is the source of life and our hope for the future. In the light of this genuine and new identity which God gives those who constitute the one body of Jesus Christ, Christians must challenge and remind all South Africans that their racial, ethnic and cultural identities are not absolute but relative, in the ongoing divine recreative activity which aims at transforming men and women into a new creation. And should Christians remain faithful in their calling and thereby succeed in relativizing the sin of racial pride and dethroning the god of racism in South Africa, they would certainly have achieved a major victory for human relations, thus laying a good foundation on which a just and humane society might be created.

Another by-product of the racial conflict in South Africa is white fear for the black majority. For *Apartheid* has succeeded in isolating various sections of society, thus providing a fertile ground for the creation of myths, half-truths and stereotypes between the racial groups. Believing that different racial groups pose mortal dangers to one another, white South Africans reel under a paralysing fear of their racially and culturally different neighbours, especially if they are blacks. The fact that such black neighbours might be Christians makes no difference. Therefore, out of sheer fear whites have created a 'golden calf', namely *Apartheid*, which promises them life and security as well as future survival as a racial group. Christians are people who know and live in the truth that sets them free (John 8.32). Indeed, seeking to be Christians in a racially divided South Africa involves a prophetic ministry, one of continuously reminding people that Christians have not received the calling to worship and to be terrorized by uncontrollable fears, and certainly not the fears of their racially different neighbours. For, as Paul, with deep insight, reminds us, because Christians are people who in Christ have been adopted sons and daughters, they have not received the spirit that makes them slaves to fear (Rom. 8.15). Therefore, being a Christian in South Africa means that one is called upon to struggle against the fear that has enslaved white people in order to exorcise and overcome it. Indeed, seeking to be Christian in South Africa challenges Christians to embody the biblical message, namely, that God's people have not been thrown upon their own devices to secure and save themselves in God's world. For God has promised to stand by, surround, defend and sustain and redeem God's people now and in the future. It is for this reason that God gave Jesus for our world and for us as a pledge that God is and will be for us. Because the Holy Spirit is actively engaged in evoking faith in this living God in whose hands our lives are more than safe now and in the future, Christians can relativize and strip fear of its paralysing and enslaving power by proclaiming to South Africans that it is not fear but God the Creator and Saviour who has the last word over God's people. In so doing, Christians would be calling South Africans to have the courage to be, to live and work creatively in our richly endowed land, the land which is decorated by its Creator with the racial and cultural diversity which should be valued as a source of enrichment and challenge for its citizens to experiment with new forms or interpersonal rela- tionships. Should Christians succeed in the task of relativizing fear while at the same helping to awaken a genuinely liberative faith in them, they would have enabled South Africans to be truly human in their unlimited openness to one another and to the challenges that confront them.[8]

Notes

1. See *The Kairos Document: Challenge to the Church* (revised edition), Johannes- burg 1986, 1f.

2. For a lucid discussion of colonial theology see Victorio Araya, *God of the Poor*, Maryknoll 1987, 27f.; Jack Nelson-Pallmeyer, *The Politics of Compassion*, Maryknoll 1986, 19.

3. Quoted by Carter Lindberg, '"Through a Glass Darkly". A History of the Church's Vision of the Poor and Poverty', *The Ecumenical Review* 33, 1981, 37.

4. It might seem surprising that I should still refer to the *Apartheid* system when South Africa is supposed to be undergoing a fundamental change into the so-called new non-racial South Africa. It is uncertain what sort of creature this will be, but life for the majority of blacks has not changed. Hence we still have poor townships and homelands in a country which is so richly endowed.

5. Because *Apartheid* strikes at the heart of Christian teaching, many concerned Christians in South Africa spared no effort to fight against it. This ultimately led to the declaration that it is heresy. For a detailed discussion of the heretical nature of *Apartheid* see John de Gruchy and Charles Villa-Vicencio (eds.), *Apartheid is a Heresy*, Cape Town 1983. See also Per Frostin's perceptive essay 'Apartheid as Idolatry', in *Liberation Theology in Tanzania and South Africa*, Lund 1988, 104–36.

6. Desmond Tutu, 'Apartheid and Christianity', in *Apartheid is a Heresy* (n. 5), 46f.

7. Quoted ibid., 45.

8. Simon S. Maimela, 'Man in White Theology', *Journal of Theology for Southern Africa* 36, September 1981, 30–41.

III · The Social and Political Dynamics of Africa after the End of the Political Presence of the Soviet Union

Andrea Riccardi

'Millions of people in Africa could die over the next few months', commented the Director General of UNICEF, pointing out how the continent was facing a dramatic crisis. The images of death and famine in the Horn of Africa in 1984–85, with almost two million dead, still remain in the collective memory. But today perhaps international public opinion is less attentive to the problems and the misery of the African continent. The Gulf crisis has aggravated the precarious economic situation of Africa and heightened its economic vulnerability, while emergency aid to the USSR and the Eastern European countries is absorbing Western energies and making people forget the problems of Africa. A logical critique of co-operation between North and South – sometimes made for ulterior motives – has weakened the West's sense of responsibility for the African continent. It is no exaggeration to say that Africa is the forgotten entity in the international community.

Moreover, the voice of Africa is extremely faint on the international scene because of so many more pressing messages. Africa has only 1% of the press and television networks of the world, and those it has, often operate in conditions of little freedom (two-thirds of the countries of Africa south of the Sahara have less than ten newspapers each). And even if the process of democratization taking place in various countries has stimulated the national press, the voice of Africa, like the majority of reports from Africa, is silenced in the great international pool of information. So there is a risk that the African crisis will be ignored and forgotten.

This crisis has vast proportions. The continent almost seems to favour the outbreak of wars. With the end of the bipolarity between the USA and the USSR, the context in which African conflicts are developing is more uncontrolled and no less dangerous, often characterized by obscure connections which are not so much ideological as solid and anchored in specific interests. Among the great number of African conflicts one can point to at least thirteen major wars: Angola, Ethiopia, Liberia, Mali, Mauritania, Mozambique, Uganda, Ruanda, Western Sahara, Senegal, Somalia, Sudan and Chad.

In the Horn of Africa a long series of bloody conflicts seems now to have been resolved in the direction of a new political equilibrium, though in Ethiopia, Eritrea and Somalia this has not yet been defined. In southern Africa, along with the independence of the last colony, Namibia, there are positive signs of a solution to the Angolan conflict. The negotiations have led to an agreement between the government and UNITA on a democratic state; a conflict which developed with a strong ideological identity and in the framework of a regional dispute seems to be being resolved within the framework of a political confrontation. The same cannot yet be said of Mozambique, where negotiations are only being carried on between the government and RENAMO.

Something is happening in the dramatic framework of the 'thirteen African wars' and the minor conflicts going on around them. Undoubtedly the continent is no longer the scene of disputes between the two superpowers. However, ethnic, regional, tribal, economic, internal and external issues cause and stimulate bloody conflicts. The frontiers of the war permanently cross many African countries. The young generations are growing up with war, becoming accustomed to regarding it as more than a transitory episode in their lives. And in the case of Sudan, torn between an Islamic majority and an animist and Christian minority, and experiencing an interminable ethnic and religious war, a solution seems to be remote.

To a large extent the African wars affect the continent south of the Sahara (with the exception of the Western Sahara). In fact Mediterranean, Arab or Arabic-speaking Africa has a different relationship with Europe and the Middle East. This area has Islamic countries with a developed state and with strong ruling classes. In this region, although the economic framework is still uncertain, one major problem for political stability is the confrontation with religious fundamentalism. In the countries of the Maghreb, perhaps more than in Egypt, it is now by no means easy to measure the grip which the Islamic movements have on society, with their call for a refounding of the state on the basis of religious law. The near future will provide occasions for quantifying these movements, their electoral significance and the consensus they command. In this respect Algeria, unlike Egypt, is the most acute political point of conflict.

At all events the political situation of Mediterranean Africa, despite its complex links with the rest of the continent, is different from that of sub-Saharan Africa. In North Africa – and this is no small difference – there are states which have some solidarity. Moreover North Africa, because of its history and its relative strength, has a more prominent profile in international society. However, a crisis of greater proportions is affecting the black continent. Having recalled the 'African wars', I need only touch on the economic situation. Certainly the African economies are not all cursed with the same weakness, but their general framework is anything but healthy and reassuring.

The Black continent has experienced the repercussions of the Gulf crisis, and the recurrent crisis over raw materials. Its capacity for saving is zero, while African exports have dropped steeply in volume and value. When economic resources are not used for private ends (the Trilateral reckons that the flight of capital represents a third of the public debt), they are often used in a very irrational way, sometimes in construction work of virtually no public utility or in military expenditure. This is a political problem and one caused by the ruling classes.

The stereotyped image of Africa in the middle of the century was that of a producer of raw materials: from Egyptian cotton to Moroccan phosphate, to coffee, cocoa, ground nuts from West Africa, minerals, gold, diamonds, uranium . . . This was the great African treasure, which the developed North seemed to need. But above all in the 1980s the African treasure lost much of its value. The European economies are already finding substitutes for materials that until recently were considered essential, or are looking for necessities elsewhere. The prices of the African 'treasure' are fixed externally and it is calculated that sub-Saharan Africa accounts for only 1.3% of world trade. The myth of the natural treasure of Africa has given way to an awareness of the great weakness of the African economies in the international sphere. 'On the casino of raw materials,' Fottorino wrote in *Le Monde*, 'Africa has lost. For many people its debt is a gambling debt.'

The interventions of the World Monetary Fund and the World Bank compel national economies to take severe measures to regain equilibrium. The effects of these measures are not seen in the short term, but the sacrifices they demand are obvious. Sub-saharan Africa often survives thanks to humanitarian, political and diplomatic aid towards democratic development, so often linked to a 'good vote' at the UN. The democratic changes have raised questions, as in Benin, Ivory Coast and Gaboon, about the function of state and para-state administrations, which often cause economic paralysis. In Cameroon the number of those employed in public administration has grown from 51,340 to 101,194 in ten years, between 1971 and 1981.

But the process of economic reconstruction is so difficult that no one believes that Africa can achieve this by itself. There is a need to develop a new culture of international solidarity and incisive action in the most delicate sectors. The Second Conference of the Under-Developed Countries, held in Paris in October 1990, noted that the forty-one states involved (twenty-eight of them African) accounted for about 1% of world trade. If the perhaps rather simplistic idea of a 'Marshall plan' for Africa has been put forward, it is also necessary for Europe to want to avoid landing itself with the consequences of a continental crisis, as is evident from the phenomenon of mass migration. At the end of 1990, in Lagos, at the World Conference on Reparations for Africa and Africans in the Diaspora, the idea was put forward of reparations owed by Europe and America to the black continent for the 'long night of the slave trade', to use the Prime Minister of Benin's phrase.

These are strong ideas aimed at reviving an international culture of solidarity with Africa, which today is largely in crisis, at a time when Western attention is turned towards the East and there is a feeling of closer ties with the ex-communist world. The changes taking place in the African countries do not merit less attention than those in the Eastern European countries. However, they receive little space in the media, and do not enthuse public opinion in the same way as '1989'.

The Africa of wars, of economic crisis, of proverbially unstable political power (thirty-seven *coups d'état* have been counted between 1963 and 1982), is a continent undergoing a profound evolution. One need only cite events in South Africa, the crisis of *Apartheid*, which offers hope of a positive outcome from a racist system from which no one saw any way out. This is a complex evolution in the African state. The single party, after more or less brief spells of a multi-party system, had been the usual instrument of government, the link between state and society. Often the party was identified with the head of state.

Theories about this political situation varied enormously. Some emphasized the distinctive character of African society and the incompatibility between a multi-party régime and the traditional idea of power. On the other hand, however, the single party basically legitimated itself by pointing to the ideological Marxist-Leninist option, which related the single-party systems in Africa to those of the Socialist countries. The crisis of the socialist régimes and the 'Gorbachev effect' have made themselves felt in the African countries, sometimes revealing power structures in the style of Ceaucescu.

The fortunes of Marxism-Leninism in Africa had risen not only as a result of Soviet influence (countries which adopted this ideology often had links with the USSR) but also because the ideology bound the nascent African states together. The ideological factors had a fundamental role, providing a rationale for a centralized and authoritarian power, a centralized economy tied to a plan, and exalting the revolutionary character of national politics. Moreover, Marxism-Leninism did not come from the old colonial powers. The current ideological crisis is causing remarkable political problems among the ruling classes.

Evolution in systems of government has been very rapid in recent years, even if it has not attracted attention proportionate to the changes that have taken place. Just a year ago, only five countries out of forty-six in black Africa were ruled over by a democratic-type system: Gambia, Senegal, Botswana, Mauritius and Namibia, the state which has most recently become independent. Countries as different in both their international profile and internal structure as the Kenya of Arap Moi and the Zimbabwe of Mugabe seemed rooted in a single-party system for various reasons. But the multi-party system and democracy have ended up establishing themselves, albeit problematically, in almost all the African states – under the thrust of domestic opinion, guerrilla movements or the pressure of non-African countries. One example has been the transition of Benin from a system of Marxist-Lenist dictatorship, after seventeen years of a military régime, to free elections, with an important transitional phase in which the church has played a role. This example has encouraged other countries on the way of democratization. At Capo Verde, for the first time in Africa, as a result of free presidential elections, an opposition leader has come to power through the popular vote. The rulers of the small archipelago of Sao Tome e Principe have learned from experience and, after fifteen years of power exercised in close connection with Cuba and East Germany, have not stood for re-election. In Mozambique the government entered into negotiations with RENAMO, an armed opposition movement, and to this degree began a process of democratization in the country.

It is impossible here to follow the complex and slow evolution of the various African countries: the Ivory Coast, a model country of French colonization, with President Houphouet-Boigny as its head on independence, is in the depths of economic crisis and after a long period of disorder has opted for a multi-party system. Democratic elections are planned in Cameroon within a year, here too as a result of popular and student pressure. Gaboon and the Congo are also taking this line. Madagascar has rediscovered a free press and a pluralistic system, while a strong opposition movement is developing and is moving towards a determined confrontation with the government in what is for the moment a peaceful way, supported by a mass consensus.

In West Central Africa, Ghana, Equatorial Guinea, Mauritania and Central Africa seem to have remained immune to the thrust toward pluralism. In Mauritania this has been demonstrated by Saddam Hussein, who invested a good deal in the country. The president of Ghana has declared that 'the idea of a civil government . . . is a colonial legacy'. Burundi and Ruanda (where free elections are planned within a year) are in the grips of violent ethnic explosions; in Tanzania there is a move towards economic but not yet towards political liberation. Elections in Niger are planned for 1992; in Zambia, consultations are timetabled for October 1991. The military régimes of Nigeria, Guinea and Lesotho are now moving towards a civil government.

One particularly stubborn situation until recently has been that in Zaire, where in twenty-three years of exclusive reign Mobutu had based his authority on the single party in which everyone was enrolled from birth and on a movement of African 'authenticity' which gave the régime its ideological basis. Now the country seems to be moving towards a multi-party system, albeit within certain limits. In Zambia, too, where the one-party system seemed solid, the situation is being discussed again. In Zimbabwe the government was based on a democratic process involving free elections, which had seen confrontation between and regrouping of a variety of historical forces: Mugabe had subsequently inclined towards a system based on a single party, which he judged to be more suited to the nature and development of the country. But now there are signs of rethinking.

This dry and summary list of changes, largely incomplete, does not bring out the different character of the processes of democratization in the various African countries and the different motivations behind them. One cannot foresee a positive outcome for all of them, but the phenomenon is a massive one. Without doubt '1989' has exercised a profound influence in Africa. This is a thrust which comes from a distance, as a result of the crises of ideological models and political cultures. Moreover Africa is concerned to give itself a new look in its relations with the West. But above all one cannot fail to note the malaise which is widespread in many African countries in connection with state government and public affairs. The corruption, the economic difficulties, the decline in urban living conditions, the confusion between party and state, between public and private, are putting pressure on the search for new forms of state. The great impetus for change comes from within African society.

Rebuilding the state involves facing the problems of different races and different religious groups. For example, in Nigeria, which has started on a process of democratization, an attempted *coup d'état* has again brought out the conflict between the races of the north and those of the south, between Christians and Muslims. The majority of African states are not homogeneous even in religious terms. This characteristic alone poses a serious problem for the identity of the state.

Apart from Somalia, the Comoro Islands and Mauritania, where Islam is absolutely dominant, elsewhere Muslim majorities live side by side with Christian minorities, as in Senegal (90% Muslim), Mali (75%), Guinea (70%) and Niger (88%). Catholicism predominates in Ruanda (56%), Burundi (79%), Zaire (48%), Angola (69%) and Equatorial Guinea (72%); Protestantism in South Africa (46%). The rest of Black Africa has a dominantly animist population (which is not easy to quantify), with obviously variable Christian and Muslim elements. Gigantic Nigeria, with almost 117 million inhabitants, has a slight Islamic majority. Sudan, which is predominantly Muslim (73%), has a Christian and animist south which is resisting the imposition of the Islamic law.

As compared to four states which are Islamic by confession, the majority of the countries are secular: but the relationship between governments and religious confessions has not always been easy to work out, whether because of the weakness of the state and its concern to impose itself on society, or because of the power of the confessional organizations and their institutions. Some African countries have had a policy of discrimination against the churches, but now this seems largely to be under review. This is evident in the case of Benin, where a Catholic bishop has been called to preside over the national assembly and to safeguard the transition: this example has been followed in Gaboon, and elsewhere clergy have been involved in peace negotiations, as for example in Mozambique.

The construction of a secular and multi-religious state poses a great problem in a society which needs to call on all possible internal and international resources. Of course in Arabic-speaking Mediterranean Africa the problem takes on a very different aspect. Here the Christian presence is extremely small, and is often made up of non-native elements who are considered guests in 'Dar-al-Islam'. The only significant exception is Egypt, where the Coptic minority of the Patriarchate of Alexandria represents a striking and original Christian presence, which is very critical of the Islamicization of the state.

The changes in Africa are deeper than international public opinion realizes. Of course the media have followed the changes in South Africa with greater attention. Here too a solution is a long way off, with 8000 dead in four years as a result of inter-racial conflicts. The ANC is engaged in building itself up as a party. But the political game is very complex. The building of a new South Africa with 35 million inhabitants, 80% of which are black and 14% white, is proving very difficult, more so than the dismantling of *Apartheid*. The end of the isolation of the country highlights the role that could be played by the government and South African entrepreneurs in a continental economy in need of aid and investment. South Africa exports 32% of its manufactured goods to countries on the continent and now has commercial relations with all the African states. The economic crisis of the continent requires South Africa to play a major role, while domestically the country has to reconstruct itself politically in very difficult conditions.

The Africans are working hard for change in this phase, despite the low level of information and the lack of study centres. Ideas are circulating in an atmosphere of anxiety about novelty and change. But the basic structural framework remains very oppressive. It is forecast that in twenty years the population of Africa will reach one billion, with a food shortage of dramatic proportions. Probably – and this is another sign of decay – the demographic growth will be affected negatively by the spread of AIDS, which may well produce a decline in the population of some countries.

The international conference on AIDS held in Kinshasa in 1990 had indicated the gravity of the danger, and this has been amply confirmed in subsequent months. WHO estimates that around five million people in Africa are HIV positive, and forecasts double that for 1992. It is calculated that between 8% and 10% of the populations of the major cities of Central and East Africa are HIV positive.

To this African 'scourge' is added that of the high number of refugees, which gives the continent another sad 'first', that of the world's greatest producer of refugees. Mozambique has exported a million and a half refugees, Liberia 550,000. It is calculated that in the Horn of Africa there are more than three and a half million refugees. There are some 200,000 from Burundi and 310,000 from Angola. One cannot help thinking about the future of a continent which today – and this is a new phenomenon over the last ten years – is becoming a centre for drug traffic and production. The cultivation of some drugs is gaining ground on cocoa, coffee, cotton, etc. As a result of this phenomenon there is a risk of mass intoxication among the populace uprooted from the country and urbanized, which has lost the ties of clan and family solidarity. The spread of the very different types of drug has been facilitated by the lack of any awareness of self-defence. An agricultural revolution in drugs is convulsing whole areas of Africa, affecting the life of its inhabitants and making this a raw spot in world trade.

The revolution in the traditional worlds over the past thirty years has come about through a process of highly accelerated urbanization, of the kind often to be found in the Third World. This phenomenon has devastated local economies and clan and tribal identities, creating an

African individual who as it were thinks and lives in quite a new context, anthropologically remote from that of his immediate past and his family. Between 25% and 50% of the population of Zaire, Ghana, the Ivory Coast, Cameroon, Liberia, Senegal and Somalia lives in cities.

As a symbol of modernity in Africa, the African city to a high degree expresses the contradiction in African society: it brings together different populations and forces, but does not integrate them; it confronts them with models of opulent life, at levels which they cannot attain. It is often the capital, the pride of the state, which is a mirage for the populations of the interior. In the African city, life is not easy for the majority of people; but even more problematical is the government of an urban mass outside the traditional frameworks.

These problems again bring up the question of the state and its relationship to society. But what can an African state do when confronted with such 'cataclysms'? What can it do when confronted with the interests of the multi-nationals? This African state does not have the chance to stand up for itself in the context of international aid. From the 1960s onwards, Africa has experienced the great period of national independence, then discovered its intrinsic and external limits. Faced with the dramatic framework of the situation, but also the energies which have been unleashed in spite of everything, it is basically trying to rethink the significance of independent nationhood propped up by international cooperation. But perhaps above all through the Western world, it is now time for it to discover more radically its own interdependence. An old historical debt – one need only think of the slave trade – obliges the non-African world again to think and practise a solidarity with this continent where, despite everything, there is a great impetus towards change.

Translated by John Bowden

IV · A Critical Review of the *Lineamenta* on the Special African Synod

Justin S. Ukpong

Introduction

Following the announcement by Pope John Paul II on 6 January 1989 to convene a Special Assembly for Africa of the Synod of Bishops, the *Lineamenta* (outline) for preparing for this synod was promulgated at the SECAM[1] general assembly in Lome in July 1990. The theme of the synod – 'The Church in Africa and Her Evangelizing Mission Towards the Year 2000: "You shall be my witnesses" (Acts 1.8)' – is presented in the *Lineamenta* as follows: first there is a brief history of the evangelization of Africa, followed by Part One of the main presentation which deals with the meaning and necessity of evangelization; next is Part Two, which identifies and analyses five different 'tasks' of evangelization in Africa, namely: Proclamation of the Good News of Salvation, Inculturation, Dialogue, Justice and Peace, and Means of Social Communications. The *Lineamenta* concludes with a questionnaire on each of the above five 'tasks' of evangelization.

The purpose of this article is to appraise the *Lineamenta* presentations on the above topics from the perspective of the African church experience, and raise issues for further discussion. I shall seek to bring out the philosophical, theological and methodological assumptions that frame each presentation. Thus my focus is not only on what the *Lineamenta* says but also, and most importantly, on the assumptions that lie behind what it says, and the methodological presuppositions of the presentation. This article has seven sections. The first section, entitled 'Background', evaluates the presentation on the history of the evangelization of Africa, and the meaning and necessity of evangelization. Sections 2–6 evaluate the presentations on the five different 'tasks' of evangelization. The last section is an overall appraisal.

1. Background

The main discussion in the *Lineamenta* is prefaced by a brief history of the evangelization of Africa and a clarification of the concept of evangelization.

Clearly the concept of history as *magistra vitae* (teacher of life) underlies the historical presentation. This is the concept which sees history as a retelling of the past in order to learn lessons for the present. On it is based the idea of history repeating itself. Also, the approach to history as the story of the victors is very evident. There is a deep impression of the defeat of Christianity and the triumph of Islam. In view of the fact that the theme of the synod is the future evangelization mission of the African church, this approach is not very helpful. The history of the evangelization of Africa ought to be presented in such a way as to provide the proper vision, inspiration and commitment needed for the African church to create a new history in the third millennium. For it is to be noted that history is not a presentation of dead facts but a matter of interpretation of facts; the purpose of the interpretation determines the selection and organization of facts and their interpretation. Moreover, history is created by human beings participating in events; it does not just happen. And history repeats itself where knowledge of past events has not been utilized to create new situations.

The church in North Africa flourished and then dwindled away. The early attempts to evangelize West Africa did not meet with lasting success. Today the church is flourishing in sub-Saharan Africa. First of all, instead of interpreting the North African story as a defeat of Christianity, we should interpret it from a forward-looking perspective which involves looking beyond the obvious to the less apparent for historical meaning. This means that we should not interpret it as the story of the victors but as the story of the victims seen as possible real heroes. This is the paradigm of the historical meaning of the passion-resurrection event whereby Jesus, the 'victim' of death in human eyes, was in actual fact the victor-hero. The struggle of North African Christians to maintain the faith should be highlighted. This struggle brought about the survival of the Coptic and Ethiopic churches, which have managed to weather the storm of Muslim aggression till today.

Secondly, we should see a connection between the North African story and today's sub-Saharan African stories. We should look on the church in North Africa as having accomplished a mission, and its 'demise' as a symbol of the seed of Christianity sown in African soil which is sprouting and flourishing today in sub-Saharan Africa. In this way African Christians south of the Sahara can claim in a historical sense to be heirs to the Christian heritage. In this way, too, the need will be seen to take the realities of the church in Africa today seriously as the raw material for creating the type of a new history that we want.

With regard to the concept and necessity of evangelization, in Africa today the question is less a matter of clarifying these concepts than identifying the type of evangelization needed in the light of the actualities of the African situation. Africa today needs evangelization that is integral and dialogical. It should be 'integral' in the sense that the gospel message should permeate all aspects of the people's life – religious, economic, political, cultural, social, etc. This implies a theology of evangelization that holds in creative tension the material and spiritual aspects of the people's lives and looks on them as complementary. 'Dialogical' is opposed to monological, and means that evangelization should be concerned not only with giving the Christian message to a people but also with how the people's context shapes the interpretation of Christianity and its message.

2. Proclamation of the good news of salvation

Against the backdrop of competing proclamations of the gospel by different religious sects in Africa today, authentic proclamation of the gospel is rightly emphasized as the most essential task of evangelization. However, I miss the mention of certain elements which are vital to such proclamation. First is the fact that Jesus Christ himself is the good news of salvation, and was also the first proclaimer of the good news. This calls for the centrality of Jesus and of the Bible in the proclamation and in the lives of Christians. Jesus must be seen as the paradigm of our proclamation. We must constantly ask what Jesus' attitude was towards certain issues, persons, situations, etc. Unless the centrality of Jesus is recognized both in what is preached and in the life-style of the preacher, we run the risk of not preaching 'the truth of the gospel' (Gal. 1.14).

Authentic proclamation also demands that recipients of the gospel message be seen as an important factor in the proclamation process. As a category, recipients are not mere passive objects but active participants in the proclamation process who may not be treated as *tabula rasa*. This raises the need to take into account not only their background but also their contribution in the hermeneutical process of appropriating the message of salvation. Today Christianity has entered a new phase of its life in Africa. Basic to this new phase is that Africa is no longer to be considered as the *object* but as the *subject* of evangelization. This is more than saying that Africans have become *agents* of evangelization. It is saying that Africa is no longer to be seen as a land out there to be conquered with the gospel message read through the lenses of another culture, but as a land that is also heir to the patrimony that is the gospel message, which it must appropriate with its own resources. This implies for the African church a search for authentic Christian self-definition and authentic interpretation and expression of Christianity, and in turn the setting free of the Christian message for appropriation and interpretation by African Christians.

Authentic proclamation also implies addressing contemporary issues. Hence the need to identify the pressing religious, economic, social and political issues facing Africa today as challenges calling for the prophetic voice of the church.

Finally, the African Synod must face the question of how to tap the human and material resources in Africa and organize them towards indigenous growth in evangelization. Let me pose a question to clarify the point: How many new insights have the local churches in Africa brought to its task of evangelization in recent years in view of the large numbers of trained local clergy, with respect to, for example, writing new catechisms, organizing parish structures that respond to current needs of the situation, restructuring the ministry, the liturgy, the rituals, etc.[2]

3. Inculturation

The presentation on inculturation rightly links inculturation with the biblical mandate to evangelize all peoples (nos. 46, 47) and traces the genesis of its practice to apostolic and ecclesiastical traditions. However, in the analysis this basic insight and its hermeneutical implications are not sufficiently followed through.

First of all, inculturation is understood in the text in terms of the gospel influencing cultures only; there is no indication that it also involves bringing new dimensions to the understanding of the gospel. Thus in the encounter between gospel and culture (process of inculturation), only culture is supposed to be 'transformed' and made to accept Christianity (no. 47), and criteria are established for determining what cultural values may be assumed into Christian practice (nos. 50, 51). Nothing is said about a possible reinterpretation of the gospel message in the light of a new cultural experience. The text actually mentions instances of such reinterpretation in the New Testament (no. 47), but does not utilize the insight hermeneutically. For their hermeneutical importance in this context, two incidents in the New Testament deserve mention. First is the admission of Gentile Cornelius into the church without circumcision (an important case of inculturation). This entailed not only conversion on Cornelius' part but also a reinterpretation of the Christian faith on the part of Peter and the other apostles for whom this had hitherto been unthinkable. The second is the fact that in the New Testament we find not only a Jewish but also a Hellenistic interpretation of the one Jesus.[3]

The relation between faith and culture is expressed in the text in terms of faith taking 'from culture those elements which are suitable to illustrate her mysteries, while culture seeks to appropriate to herself the truths revealed, at times through a tiring effort' (no. 50). In view of an earlier reference to inculturation as a 'synthesis between culture and faith' (no. 48), is the relation between faith and culture not better seen in terms of faith influencing and challenging culture from within, and culture influencing the interpretation and expression of faith? The two approaches have different practical consequences. For inculturation understood in the former approach, it is enough to interpret the Christian faith from a foreign perspective and then select from African culture, for the purpose of inculturation, only those elements that fit that perspective of expressing the Christian faith. For the latter approach, the totality of African culture is exposed to the Christian faith, which in the process causes the dead wood in the culture to fall apart, while authentic cultural insights help to shape the interpretation and expression of faith. Thus faith influences culture, while culture also influences the interpretation of faith, and culture does not just struggle to appropriate divine truths but rather opens itself to be totally influenced by faith. The exercise does not take place in the abstract (against the impression given in the former approach) but in concrete human communities and in individuals.

Next, I would like to ask: is evangelization really 'inconceivable without inculturation' (no. 47)? Would it not be more correct to say that evangelization is inconceivable without *some measure* of inculturation? Or better, that effective evangelization demands inculturation? For, if evangelization were inconceivable without inculturation and inculturation was defined as 'the encounter of the Good News with all people of the earth through the *instrumentality* of their culture' (no. 47, emphasis mine), we would not be debating inculturation in sub-Saharan Africa today after about a century of continuous evangelization. The true position is that the gospel was announced to Africa through the framework of European culture, while only those elements of African culture that fitted into that framework were taken on board in the process. African culture as such was not really considered or utilized as an *instrument* of evangelization. Attempts were even made to have it replaced by European culture, which was considered better and 'Christian'.

Since inculturation is perhaps the most significant issue on which the African church today has made some progress, the need is felt to present in broad outline in the *Lineamenta* the state of the question here as a means of raising consciousness about future expectation. Such a presentation would help to shape the direction of the analysis. The need for this is not superseded by the invitation to episcopal conferences to write about their efforts in this matter. It would rather have provided the framework for presenting such information.

Regarding the New Testament foundations for inculturation, it is important to mention the example of Jesus, who used the Jewish culture to present the Good News; and the letter to the Galatians, where Paul argues that Gentiles need not adopt a Jewish cultural identity in order to be Christians.

Finally, I find the presentation on inculturation as a whole not sufficiently forward-looking. So far the practice of inculturation in Africa has remained mostly at the level of peripheral liturgical adaptation. The issue to occupy the Synod Fathers should be how to move beyond this.

Inculturation has serious implications for both the African church and the church universal. It means that the church's life and thought are no longer to be thought of in monolithic terms but in terms of a diversity of cultures. This implies the affirmation, in practical terms, of the cultural identities of peoples within the universal church and the empowerment of these peoples to interpret and express Christianity differently in their lives. It implies, too, the movement of churches hitherto at the periphery to the centre of the life and activity of the church universal, so that the universality of the church is expressed in terms of a communion of churches, and a sharing of power in collegiality rather than in terms of uniformity and conformity to one pattern.

Fully implemented, inculturation involves a challenge and a risk – a challenge to the local churches to define their authentic self-image, and the risk of the boat of the church's universality (as this has been hitherto understood) being rocked in the process. Karl Rahner's theological analysis of our epoch (that of a transition from European to world church) as being parallel to the transition from Jewish to Gentile Christianity, with the crises this involved, is very helpful here.[4]

4. Dialogue

The presentation acknowledges dialogue as a means for the church to fulfil its mandate to preach the gospel to all creation and analyses the circumstances of dialogue at different levels arranged according to the 'concentric circles' concept of dialogue partners. It seeks to point to the challenges of dialogue in Africa at each level.

Unfortunately, the text nowhere proffers a definition of dialogue. And when we pose the question, 'dialogue for what?', no amount of teasing the text yields a substantive answer. This makes it difficult to form a clear image of the reality discussed and the perspective of discussion. Here I shall adopt a working definition that will guide our discussion. Based on Pope John Paul II's definition of inter-religious dialogue,[5] I see dialogue in this context as an approach in relating with *other* people which assumes the freedom and legitimacy of these people to be themselves and which promotes understanding and respect for them even in their faith situation. The purpose of dialogue is to learn and be enriched by knowledge of the *other* and not to force change on the *other* or confront the *other* with advantage.

One significant factor that has given rise to the practice of dialogue in the church today which the text omits is the de-emphasis, on the part of the church, of a triumphalist self-image, informed by an ecclesiology that sees the church as always needing reform and self-evangelization. Vatican II speaks of the Catholic church sharing in the blame of Christian disunity (*Unitatis Redintegratio*, no. 3). Dialogue is possible only when the *other* is regarded as a partner and not as an addressee.

I find inaccurate the statement that 'without dialogue the Church cannot proclaim the Good News' (no. 55). If in practice this were so, then dialogue would not have been a modern issue. The fact that the good news has been proclaimed in Africa for over a century and we are only discussing dialogue now is proof that the good news can be proclaimed without dialogue. It would, however, be more accurate to say that evangelization by its nature calls for dialogue, and that any approach to evangelization that is not dialogical is inadequate.

In the identification of the different levels of dialogue I miss the level of intra-ecclesial dialogue. This is dialogue within the church itself – among the hierarchy, clergy and religious, and between these and the laity.

In my opinion, the analysis of dialogue with African traditional religion misses the central point which makes this dialogue different from dialogue with other non-Christian religions. African traditional religion is an integral part of the African world-view, and it is basically what informs the day-to-day existence of average African Christians. Today the average African Christian is torn apart between the African and the Christian world-views. The primary purpose of dialogue here is the integration of the two world-views so as to give the African Christian an integrated religious personality. In this context dialogue takes place first and foremost in the minds of individual Christians; it is basically non-verbal. This is the most fundamental level of this dialogue, and the issue is how to help Christians, not just neophytes and catechumens, to engage in this dialogue. At another level this involves formal study and analysis of this religion; at another level still it involves interaction with its practitioners.

In the analysis of the different levels of dialogue it is evident that the institutional model of dialogue rather than the people-of-God model is the framework used. I find this unsatisfactory. The institutional model conceives of dialogue primarily, though not exclusively, in terms of relations between institutions (i.e. the Catholic Church as an institution and other institutions or systems), while the 'people of God model' conceives of dialogue primarily in terms of interaction between people belonging to these institutions.

That the institutional model is what informs the analysis is clear from the fact that when it comes to analysing dialogue with African traditional religion there is the problem of finding an institution as partner (no. 69). Also, the text consistently speaks of the church being in dialogue, and there is no doubt that the institutional church is meant. Besides, the 'concentric circle' approach to identifying dialogue partners, whereby the Coptic and Ethiopic Orthodox Churches are seen as the closest neighbours, is meaningful only in the institutional framework. In the 'people of God framework', the focus is on individual Catholics as participants in dialogue. And some African Catholics have practitioners of the traditional religion or Muslims or Protestants as their closest neighbours, and may never have seen Coptic or Ethiopic Christians. In this framework, therefore, it is not possible to speak of one group, particularly the Coptic and Ethiopic Christians, as the closest neighbours.

While the institutional model is suitable for analysing dialogue at the level of the universal church, which is the context of pope Paul VI's *Ecclesiam Suam*, it is a very poor candidate at the level of the local church, which is the focus of the *Lineamenta*. For, of its nature, the institutional model implies that dialogue is verbal, formal and structured, while at the level of the local church, which is concerned with the grassroots, dialogue is more often than not informal, unstructured and non-verbal. This explains why even though different forms of dialogue are identified early on in the text and in spite of the fact that dialogue is acknowledged to go beyond structures, in the analysis itself these insights are not brought in. For example, about 80% of African Catholics live in rural communities where relationships are close, and one may find people belonging to three or four different dialogue groups (namely, practitioners of African traditional religion, Protestants, Muslims, Catholics) in one community. Some forms of dialogue involve the interaction of people from all these groups together at the same time, e.g. when finding common solutions to the community's problems. This is the most rudimentary and functional form of inter-religious dialogue in Africa, but it does not have any place in the analysis.

In the light of the fact that dialogue has not made much progress in Africa and yet African society is religiously pluralistic, the *Lineamenta* presentation of this very important aspect of the Church's mission should have a sharp focus geared towards giving inspiration and a sense of direction and commitment in this matter. Discussions on dialogue today have advanced beyond the stage of the Vatican II euphoria of discovering the Protestants as our separated brethren and other religions as somehow related to the church, to analysing the modality, grounds and goals of dialogue, and in the case of non-Christian religions, evaluating them theologically. It should be considered a major task of the synod to interpret the meaning of these religions in the light of God's universal saving activity in history. The pluralistic nature of African society should stand us in good stead in making a meaningful and original contribution in this matter.

5. Justice and peace

That action in respect of justice and peace is constitutive of evangelization, and the implications of this for the mission of the church in Africa, make up the focus of the *Lineamenta* presentation on this topic. In the presentation there is concern for theological soundness evidenced in the biblical analysis and exposition of the church's teachings, and for stock-taking of where Africa is in the practice of justice and peace.

Because justice and peace are burning issues in Africa today, the text, in spite of its limited scope, provokes a lot of reflection. First of all with regard to the theological foundations, even though it is acknowledged that concern for human needs was bound up with Jesus' mission, there is need to state clearly and with emphasis that Jesus' practice of evangelization constitutes the paradigm for the church's evangelization activity today, and that the church's mission is a participation in, and a continuation of, Jesus' proclamation of the kingdom. Thus the kingdom of God must be seen to be no less the theme of the church's proclamation than it was of Jesus'. This leads to what we consider the central question in the biblical analysis, i.e. 'What sort of kingdom did Jesus preach?', and to the hermeneutical question, 'To what extent is the African church faithful to this?'

The central question just posed is not adequately broached in the biblical analysis in the *Lineamenta*. The biblical texts cited to show Jesus' concern for the human condition of people should have led to a presentation of the total image of Jesus the evangelizer in this respect, that is, the unifying meaning of Jesus' actions in respect of the poor, etc. We search in vain for such an image, yet this is crucial for the completeness of the analysis and for the proper development of the hermeneutic that follows.

Contrary to some contemporary popular conceptions, the kingdom that Jesus preached does not refer to something purely spiritual which has nothing to do with material things. For the Jews (one of whom Jesus was and to whom he mainly preached) there was no separation of the spiritual from the material. The kingdom that Jesus preached signified the transformation of the totality of our world both in its material and spiritual aspects, which include individual conversion, human well-being (spiritual and temporal), the restructuring of social relations, the political order, the economic order, etc.[6] This is the programme of the mission that Jesus inaugurated and which he commanded the church, every Christian, to prosecute. Individual actions of Jesus have meaning and place within this programme.

In answering the hermeneutical question, 'To what extent is the church in Africa faithful to Christ in prosecuting this programme?', the text outlines the church's present contribution and admits, in what may be said to be an understatement, the continued presence of some worrying economic, social and political situations. The point is that there are crucial urgent problems of justice and peace in Africa today which the church must address.

If the gospel has the efficacy to transform human society as the text admits, and if these issues are still plaguing Africa in spite of the church's presence there for more than a century, it would seem that what is needed is for the church not so much to redouble its efforts as to review its approach to evangelization. The appropriate question to ask, therefore, should be: 'How do we make the good news a force to change the human lot in Africa, a force that empowers Africa's poor to respond to their situation as a challenge rather than see it as a fate to which they have to submit and about which they can do nothing?' This seems to be the crucial question that ought to occupy the synod fathers in respect of justice and peace in Africa. To answer this question effectively calls, first of all, for what may be termed, for want of a better term, a *prophetic ecclesiology*, whereby in its self-understanding the church is committed to active involvement in the lives of the oppressed and the poor, and to the promotion of and participation in the struggle for a just society as a central aspect of its mission. Secondly, it calls for a concerted programme of action at the grassroots level which, nurtured by the word of God, will turn powerless citizens into agents of change who take their future into their hands. Thirdly, it calls for a deepening of commitment to Christ in his identification with the poor and oppressed in society.

6. Means of social communications

The text points to the need for particular churches to use in evangelization the available means of social communications, both traditional and modern, and to train church personnel in communications. In the text the proliferation of radio, cinema, television and video in Africa is, in my opinion, wrongly attributed to large-scale illiteracy (no. 88). The fact is that the illiterate do not own these gadgets. The text advocates examining 'the more widely used African languages . . . to see if they can be put to use in the proclamation of the gospel message' (no. 91). I fail to see the point being made here, for African languages are already being used in African countries to proclaim the gospel message.

The use of communication tools is said to be for transmitting the 'Christian vision . . . to the African people' (no. 89). But it should also be for enabling African people to express and share their own perception of the Christian message among themselves and with others.

While the responsibility of receivers of communication to be selective is stressed (no. 92), no corresponding stress is laid on the need for communicators generally to be selective in what they put forth for public consumption. Their duty to be selective should also be stressed.

In view of the fact that the African church's participation so far in the new world communications order that is so talked about has been minimal, the synod should be seen as an appropriate occasion for launching the African church into the orbit of the new world communications order debate. Communication is a fundamental human right; it is a basic structure of society; it is at the heart of evangelization. The church should not fail to make a meaningful contribution in the discussion. A recognition of this raises certain concerns about the text under review. First of all the text focuses on the communication of the gospel only, not on communication in general as it affects the communication of the gospel. Secondly, it is interested mainly in the instrumental aspect and not in the reality of communication. Thus it does not probe into the meaning, nature and modalities of communication as a basis for the practical analysis. The church's mission is to proclaim the good news. This demands that the process of this proclamation (i.e. communication) should also be good. Thus the church's duty must start with a critique of the communication process itself. Questions that should interest the synod fathers here should include: 'How can the church influence the theories, policies and practice of communication generally and within the church in favour of the poor and the voiceless?' 'To what extent is modern mass communication concerned with human promotion?' 'How can communication be placed at the service of peace, justice and development?' 'What does the church say about the monopolization and manipulation of communication?'

It is very evident that the underlying model of communication operative in the text is the vertical one-way model whereby messages produced by a few (regarded as depositories of knowledge), and addressed to all, flow from the top downwards. This is bad communication. Today communication is being seen more as a process of exchange and sharing. When so democratized, communication fulfils its proper function in society of enhancing social existence.

If the length and depth of the text is an indication of its rating in the scale of the 'tasks' of evangelization, communication deserves better attention than it has received in the *Lineamenta*, given its importance as the most fundamental process of evangelization.

7. Final comments

One emerges from reading the *Lineamenta* with the impression of a heavy agenda for the African Synod, and a gnawing question, 'Is the synod not going to have too much on its plate?' Clearly just one of the topics in the *Lineamenta* could have sufficed as the subject matter for the synod. The fear is that the topics may not receive the attention they deserve.

All the same, the synod must be looked upon as the *kairos* of the African church – a moment to take stock of the past and to utilize that knowledge to create a new future for the church in Africa. But the Synod will not fulfil that promise unless it is seen as an occasion for African Christians to give voice to their daily struggle to clarify for themselves what it means to be church; unless that voice is given a hearing; and unless there is a critical awareness of this within the African church itself. For it must be noted that Christianity will never take roots in the hearts of Africans unless there is a struggle by African Christians themselves to understand the Christian faith and unless that struggle is encouraged.

The synod is Africa's *kairos* in another sense. It is a moment to come face to face with the issue of the irruption of the African church – the sudden entry with a great impact of the African church on to the world church scene. The challenge that this poses is enormous and calls for a paradigm-shift in the perception of what it means to be church, a search for a new way of being church, and the articulation of the need for not just a synod but for an African Council adequately to address the enormous and complex realities of the African church situation. Indeed there is need for such councils in other regions to clarify issues that have emerged since Vatican II. Such councils would be in view of a general council, to wit, Vatican III, to be held some time in the third millennium to gather up the loose ends of the post-Vatican II era.

Notes

1. SECAM means Symposium of Episcopal Conferences of Africa and Madagascar.

2. It must be admitted that much has been done in Zaire in this respect, but not much is happening in other places beyond the introduction of traditional music into the liturgy.

3. Scholars have pointed to some christological titles in the New Testament as coming from a Palestinian background, e.g. reference to Jesus in Acts 3.13–26 as 'servant' and 'prophet' like Moses; and others as coming from a Gentile Hellenistic background e.g. the title *Soter* (saviour). For an overview discussion on this, see Leopold Sabourin, *Christology: Basic Texts in Focus*, New York 1984.

4. Cf. Karl Rahner, 'Basic Theological Interpretation of the Second Vatican Council', *Theological Investigations*, Vol. 20, New York and London 1981, 77–89.

5. Cf. the 'Address of the Pope at the Conclusion of the Plenary Assembly of the Secretariat', in *The Attitude of the Church Towards the Followers of other Religions: Reflections and Orientations on Dialogue and Mission*, Secretariatus Pro Non Christianis, Rome 1984, p. 4.

6. There must be no confusion between Jesus' statement, 'my kingdom is not of this world' (John 18.36), and the 'kingdom of God' preached by Jesus. For while Jesus preached the transformation of our world as an indication of God's reign over the world, he did not in any way set himself up as an earthly king.

V · The Expectations of the Other Churches

The Expectations of the Catholic Church

René Luneau

When in September 1977, at Abidjan, the Fabian Fr Eboussi Boulaga of Cameroon formulated the desire for an African council publicly and for the first time,[1] he immediately aroused an interest among a number of churches throughout the world which has not slackened since then. Perhaps we might recall that in June 1978 Fr Yves Congar thought it worth producing a brief and very learned note as an opportune reminder that during the nineteenth and twentieth centuries there had been a number of precedents, from the twelve provincial or plenary councils held at Baltimore (USA) between 1791 and 1884 to the plenary councils of Australia (1844, 1869, 1887), China, Japan (1924), Indochina (Hanoi 1934) and India (Bangalore 1950).[2] To call for a council to be held in Africa was in fact to link up with a church tradition which for the moment was dormant.

Nor should there be any surprise that the convening by Pope John Paul II of a Special Assembly of the Synod of Bishops for Africa on 6 January 1989 immediately aroused the interest of other churches. As B. Chenu wrote in *La Croix* on 13 January 1989, 'For some years there have been dreams of a Black council. John Paul has just announced an African synod. This event should be a milestone on the way towards an African Christianity.' 'Your synod interests us', affirmed M. Cheza, the theologian from Louvain la Neuve, in a pastiche of a famous publicity campaign, and he expressed the desire that 'the non-African churches will show an active interest in this synod by avoiding the consequences of colonialism and, positively, by trying to promote a true partnership'.[3]

Is it surprising that such special attention is being paid to the churches of Africa? There are several reasons for this, which must be mentioned briefly here.

Nowhere else in the world is the Christian community growing so quickly as in Africa. The Catholic church alone is celebrating more than three and a half million baptisms each year, and this figure is constantly growing. In the course of the last fifteen years it will have doubled the number of its faithful,[4] and between 1993 and 1994 it will pass the figure of one hundred million baptized Christians. This is something both to rejoice about and to be alarmed at, and given the alarming demographic growth of the African continent – before 2010 its population will number a billion – it is certain that in the course of the next century, all confessions in Black Africa will play an essential role in the future of Christianity.

Now these churches, which are still young and more important each year, are poor churches, which all depend for their most obvious needs on the financial support of Rome or the ancient missionary churches. This dependence has rightly been said to be structural and not economic (thus the cost of the training of a priest is not commensurate with the resources of the community for which he is destined), and it leaves a permanent mark on relations between the churches. How can one experience a relationship of equality when this feeling of 'tutelage' from which nothing can really free you seems insuperable? So it is understandable that these same churches, perpetually given assistance, will never succeed in making themselves heard by those which are better provided for and that many people, though without daring to say so, think that they have not yet come of age.[5]

Certainly this essential fragility cannot be dissociated from the social and economic crisis which marks the whole of the African continent and which seems to get worse year by year. The former Secretary-General of the Organization for African Unity (OAU), Edem Kodjo, bluntly recognized: 'Globally, reality is taking a firm grip; Africa is in the process of being rapidly marginalized.'[6] René Dumont expressed his indignation in *Pour l'Afrique, j'accuse* (1986), echoing all those works which denounce an Africa 'suffering from its own disease', 'broken down', 'strangled'.[7] And it is now difficult to counter an 'Afro-pessimism'[8] which demobilizes those who are most well-disposed towards it, a pessimism which sees Africa today as a 'continent in decline'.

The picture gets even gloomier, if possible, when one takes into account the political situation of most of the African countries south of the Sahara. How many dramas there will be, present and to come, if Benin is to succeed without too much trouble in changing from a military dictatorship to a democratic régime! Blood has flowed in Mali, Togo and Cameroon, and there is every indication that all is not over. And one has only to think of the character of everyday life in certain regions or provinces of Liberia, Sudan, Ethiopia, Somalia, Mozambique, Angola . . .

It is in this eminently difficult context that the African churches are pursuing their growth and bearing witness to the gospel. How can we fail to pay attention to them when we become aware of the gravity of the social, economic or purely human issues which they face? And these are the very churches which the pope wants to bring together in a 'Special Assembly of the Synod of Bishops'.

Those who will be writing the history of the African Synod in a few years will not fail to recall the difficulties that provoked it. In September 1990, on a flight which was taking him to Ruanda and Burundi, the pope confessed to journalists: 'The African Synod has a long history which dates from the beginning of my pontificate. The proposal for it did not come from Africans. Far from being convinced about it, they were even opposed to it. However, the idea of the Synod has remained.'[9] In fact from the beginning, and in a number of churches, the suggestion for an African Council (1977) met with considerable reserve. The English-speaking churches legitimately pointed out that they had not been consulted and that they found that they had embarked on an adventure which had been decided for them. Some West African churches suspected in principle anything that could come from Cameroon or Zaire. Again, at the end of a wide consultation, in Lagos, in July 1987, the evidence had to be faced: there was no majority for a council. So it was the personal decision of the sovereign pontiff which tilted the balance. Aware of the urgent need for the African churches to collaborate over the apostolic issues of the decades to come, and not preventing the possibility of a council that might be carried away by the majority of its members, he convened a 'Special Assembly of the Synod for Africa' (6 January 1989).

Because in Africa the will of the pope is not a topic for discussion, all the churches will be present at this synod, but not necessarily with a glad heart. The churches which wanted a council have been forced to give that up. And those which did not want anything have to prepare seriously for something that they did not expect. Hence, perhaps, the utter lack of interest shown by certain African churches, noted recently by the editorial in *New People* (Nairobi, January 1991), 'Who wants the Synod?'

We can now see how difficult a synodical assembly which is very composite and marked by a variety of religious sensibilities will find it to speak with a single voice when the time is very short and the agenda, strictly speaking, limitless.

In July 1987 the Assembly of the Symposium of Episcopal Conferences of Africa and Madagascar (SECAM), which meets every three years, spelt out precisely the main and most urgent challenges and pastoral options, namely: 1. the pursuit of a primary evangelization; 2. dialogue and good relations with Islam and the traditional religions; 3. inculturation defined as 'a profound evangelization of the African Christian . . .'; 4. justice and peace; 5. the training of pastoral agents; 6. 'unity and communion between the churches'.[10]

In spring 1989 the preparatory commission of the Synod took up the most essential of these pastoral options, omitting no. 5, 'the training of pastoral agents' (the ordinary synod of October 1990 had been devoted to that) and combining nos. 6 and 2: ecumenism is one of the privileged forms of inter-religious dialogue. In addition it included on its agenda a topic which did not figure in Lagos: 'The means of social communication in the service of evangelization'.

This is an ambitious programme, and we must ask with S. Sempore whether it does not seek to 'take on too much by assigning such panoramic themes as fields of investigation'.[11] This synod will open a new era for the churches of Africa, and perhaps it needs to touch on the essential questions of the proclamation of the gospel and its rooting in a continent uncertain of its future. But surely it is clear that a single session, even if extended by several weeks, could not get to the end of such a colossal task? Just as Vatican II discovered at a late stage that it needed three or four sessions to cope with the work it had undertaken, so I estimate that in bringing together churches which are very different as a result of their history, sensibilities, political and cultural backgrounds, the African synod will choose to programme several sessions, though here and there economic constraints will make their mark. A synodical work which did not find time to mature would destroy the credibility of the whole approach.

Need we recall that the success of this African synod will also have a bearing on other churches? 'On the other shore of the Mediterranean,' said John Paul II, 'Africa, tormented, a continent of contrast, sometimes famished, is making its presence felt more closely while vigorously proclaiming its own identity and its specific place in the concert of nations. The next special assembly of the Synod of Bishops for Africa, in communion with the universal church, will allow this continent of the future to show how the gospel in our time is an unparalleled cultural leaven in the integral development and solidarity of individuals and peoples. At the heart of the church, Africa is a creator of cultures . . .'[12] A creative Africa – it is enough to listen to some churches in Africa to know the creativity they can be capable of, provided that one appeals to their responsibility for the transmission of the faith.[13]

We have to be convinced that we need the African churches. Not only because communion between the churches is an integral part of our profession of faith, but also because, at present, they are going before us on a course which will at all events also be ours. The great equilibria of the world are changing year by year: within ten years our millennary churches will represent only a third of all the Catholic communion. As the Archbishop of Milwaukee, R. Weakland, writes, 'Our ecclesial unity will not be supported by the cultural expressions of Western civilization. The limits of the West no longer make any sense for Catholicism.'[14] We should recognize that we have some difficulty in convincing ourselves of this. The more we do convince ourselves, the more quickly our 'conversion' will come about. Perhaps the African Synod will bring us new reasons for hope.

Translated by John Bowden

Notes

1. At a colloquy organized by the Society for African Culture on the theme 'Black Civilization and Catholic Church', in *Pour un Concile Africain*, Paris 1978, 124f.

2. Y. Congar, in *Informations Catholiques Internationales* 527, June 1978, 16.

3. In *L'Actualité Religieuse dans le Monde* 70, 15 September 1989, 30.

4. See the figures provided each year by the agency Fides in Rome which *Documentation Catholique*, Paris, usually publishes in the last issue of the year.

5. Cf. R. Luneau, 'Prendre la parole, être écoutées: une tâche difficile pour les Eglises d'Afrique', in R. Luneau and P. Ladrière (eds.), *Le Retour des Certitudes*, Paris 1987.

6. E. Kodjo, *L'Occident, du déclin au défi*, Paris 1983, 216.

7. T. Diakite, *L'Afrique malade d'elle-meme*, Paris 1980; J. Giri, *L'Afrique en panne*, Paris 1986; R. Dumont and M. F. Mottin, *L'Afrique étranglée*, Paris 1980, etc.

8. 'Afro-pessimism' is fortunately denounced by the journal *Politique Africaine* and the researches at the Centre d'Études Africaines in Bordeaux. These are not the only ones.

9. In *La Documentation Catholique* 2014 (21 October 1990), 916.

10. In Pro Mundi Vita Etudes, *L'Eglise dans le Monde, Panorama* 1987.2, March 1988, 12–13.

11. S. Sempore, 'Tam-tam pour un Synode', *La Croix*, 18 January 1991.

12. Speech to the Pontifical Council for Culture (12 January 1990), in *La Documentation Catholique* 2000 (18 February 1990), 154.

13. See R. Luneau and J. M. Ela, *Voici le temps des héritiers*, Karthala 1981; R. Luneau, *Laisse aller mon peuple! Eglises africaines au delà des modèles?*, Karthala 1987.

14. R. Weakland, 'Une Eglise-Monde. Diversité des cultures et unité de foi', in *La Documentation Catholique* 1991 (7 January 1990), 35.

When will the Church in Africa become African?

Rose Zoé-Obianga

The question of holding a council or synod of the church in Africa goes back to 1962, to the congress of Catholic students in Fribourg. Since then, the idea has gained ground. So at a time when Africa in general and Cameroon in particular is making active and intense preparations, as an African Protestant woman I would like to express some of our expectations. I do so in response to Fr M. Hebga, SJ, who gave reasons why an African council should be called.[1]

Here we are, then, on the eve of this synod and on the threshold of the third millennium. The very way in which I have phrased the title of this article indicates the different feelings which come over me.[2] It is meant to be a response to the call of Pope Paul VI: 'Africans, it is now up to you to be your own missionaries.'[3]

This phrase keeps going round and round in my head; it accosts me, it perturbs me; it disturbs me to the point of becoming a fascination, an obsession, since the reality to be observed on this continent remains an enigma, not to say a contradiction – a contradiction between the theory we advance and the reality we experience. What we see seems to stem from the fact that as women and men of a continent whose characteristics have already been the object of much research not only by Africanists but also by Africans themselves, we are not living out the message of the gospel. No matter what the aspect and the sphere touched on may be, no matter what method is used, what aspect is envisaged, the analyses and studies that are made simply confirm a degrading, humiliating reality in which human dignity looks like a dream.[4]

Do we really have to remind ourselves that poverty, famine, wars, sicknesses, endemic underdevelopment, illiteracy and so on, sweeping over us like turbulent, powerful and destructive waves, are the daily lot of our peoples and particularly of women? Do we really have to remind ourselves that after baptizing women, the church does not grant them all the prerogatives attached to this sacrament? The African woman is in effect declared incompetent to perform certain services and roles which are said to be important in the church. In spite of the changes and mutations which are taking place under our eyes in civic society, women are always condemned to abject submission, to a blind and demeaning obedience. In spite of all the responsibilities which are recognized in the case of women, the negative role and impact of the myth of Eve allow and legitimize the keeping of Christian women in a state of perpetual inferiority and culpability. One has the feeling that they have not benefited from the act of redemption and salvation in the cross. So did not Christ also come to save this part of humanity in distress?

Is it not aberrant to go on considering that 'the experiences of men and women of other times and other places must serve among us and for us as the compulsory mould for the life of faith'?[5] Doesn't the African church really want to make any effort at reflection, at originality? Doesn't it want to be an agent of conscientization, and hence of change? Is it refusing, deliberately and unjustly, to join in a struggle for liberation which would also include the women who are its mothers, its sisters, its wives? So while the African man is born from a woman, nourished by her, supported and loved by her, in church he is happy to carry on in the same old way, following patterns imported from elsewhere and which continue to impress on everyone that one is of either one sex or the other – with a cynicism and a cruelty which makes one doubt the depth and the sincerity of his conversion. Is the African church so unintelligent, so unendowed, so weak and so uncreative that it is content to allow the perpetuation of structures and forms of ministry which devalue and demobilize women and indeed contribute to this perpetuation?

1. When will the church in Africa become African?

The title of this article would seem first of all to be a question. When will you become African – i.e. human, beautiful, strong, capable of positive verve and initiatives which promote the women and men of this continent? When will you cease to perpetuate the anthropological pauperization of our peoples? For how long will you be closed to a dialogue which can challenge you and thus recreate you? When will you open yourselves up to the enormity of your situation, in the face of which you are adopting an attitude which is both ambivalent and hypocritical? Isn't it in fact extraordinary that the African church, made up of men and women who are scorned, downtrodden, exploited, denied, is participating in this state of affairs, purely and simply by denying the image of God in woman in its actions and gestures? Following the fathers of the church, it does not hesitate to support ideas and positions which it would do well to abandon if it really were African Christianity. Because of a partial and partisan interpretation, it distorts certain biblical texts, thus revealing the depth of its pride and its lack of humility in the Lord. It allows the perpetuation of cleavages which mean that our societies do not manage to find their way between traditional societies and the imported models which have most marginalized women. Mary Hunt affirms that 'moral theology as presently conceived seems, paradoxically, immoral', since 'it systematically excludes half of the very people whose lives it pretends to reflect'.[6] There is a risk that it will no longer have any credibility.

2. When will the church in Africa become African!

Then the title could appear as a wish. If only the church in Africa could become African! If only it could live effectively as a participating and sharing community! We are beings in relationship. An analysis of our traditional societies has always noted that. Innumerable proverbs and sayings attest it. Now the only thinkers are men. 'Women do not think in the church, and that makes itself evident above all in moral theology.'[7] The fact is that the church is masculine, directed by its celibate men. I wish that it would listen seriously to women themselves, who are most often silent and absent, not by nature, but as the result of a negative socialization. In the life of the church, the sacrament of the eucharist is *the* symbol *par excellence* of sharing. But when we look at it, we note bitterly that the church supports divisions, introduces and emphasizes differences which it refuses to transcend. It exploits women to such a degree and so well that it makes a mock of itself by its oppression, the denial of some of its members, women in particular. Now the advantages of a communal life are evident. The present structures which are so obsolete can fall and be replaced by others which promote the specific characteristics of a community of men and women who are recognized as being equally in the image of God, baptized and confirmed. Relations of a new quality can be embarked on, thus demonstrating to the world that African Christians are the true disciples of the Lord.

James Crawford sketches out for us the vision of a non-patriarchal community in which power and authority are understood in a completely different way from the way in which they are understood at present. For this community, power would be 'the skill to act, to change' and authority would be 'the right to exercise this power'.[8] In view of what has gone before, there is still a long way to go before the participation of women with their gifts, their dynamism, their enthusiasm.

3. When the church in Africa really will become African

Finally, the title can be seen as an affirmation, a certainty. The church in Africa is in process of becoming African, given the signals that we detect here and there among the theologians, male and female, and among women and men who are really committed. Here are three of them:

(a) Women are in process of 'becoming visible'. That can be seen on three levels: their absence from academic theological circles is being made good; they are taking part in and belonging to associations like EAAT and EATWOT; they are publishing works to break their silence and to make their presence felt positively. Here are women who have braved the bans, and exercised real power.

(b) The quest for new structures automatically involves changes, the upheavals which are needed if all the members of the Christian community are to have credibility and to participate effectively. The independent churches and sects which are proliferating offer us examples of courageous plans and achievements. So it is abnormal only to accept as a universal model what are in fact models specific to a certain part of the world. We would mistrust the irruption of the secular European world into the development and we would mistrust the stratification of structures which would gain from being changed, because they do not always contain the positive values of women's liberation of women which can also rebound on African men.

(c) Theological teaching ought to take account of the linguistic aspect. When we use Bibles in European languages, they convey their androcentric character and thought-models and these alienate us more. We need to take into account the history of this continent by responding to the revolutionary ideas and theories, say, of Sheikh Anta Diop, who has demonstrated that our continent has not always been inhabited by a humiliated, denied, oppressed people. We need to take account of African religious beliefs and practices. Mercy Amba Oduyoye indicates, among other things, that the divine origin of the universe, the world (from generation to generation), forms a single community, the totality of the human person, woman as an integral part of humanity.[9] We need to take account of all the paths of liberation theology throughout the world, of all the aspects of the environment which are related to justice, peace and the safeguarding of creation.

Translated by John Bowden

Notes

1. E. Milcent, 'Pour un concile africain?', *Bulletin de Theologie Africaine* (= *BTA*) V.10, 1983, 174.

2. As will emerge from the sub-headings, in the original French the title can be seen as a question, a wish and an affirmation. Unfortunately English does not have the same flexibility [Tr.].

3. Ibid.

4. J. E. Penoukou, 'Avenir des Eglises Africaines. Questions et Reflexions (suite et fin)', *BTA* V.10, 1983, 196.

5. M. Hunt, 'Transforming Moral Theology: A Feminist Ethical Challenge', *Concilium* 182, 1985, 84.

6. Ibid.

7. Ibid., 112.

8. J. Crawford, *Non-Patriarchal Models for Community. The Search for New Community. A Bossey Seminar*, 1987, 21f.

9. M. A. Oduyoye, 'The Value of African Religious Beliefs and Practices for Christian Theology', in *African Theology en Route*, Maryknoll 1977, 109–17.

The Expectations of the Orthodox Churches

Koinidis Parthenios

The encounter of the gospel with the cultures and civilizations of all ages, following from the command which the Lord himself gave to his disciples and to the holy apostles before his ascension, has from the beginning of the Christian era prevented the church from identifying itself completely with a single people or civilization. It has thus allowed the church on the one hand to organize the proclamation of the gospel to all the world, and on the other to avoid a fatal encapsulation, considering the world simply as a bringer of evil.

This encounter between the church and the world down the centuries has, among other things, resulted in the formation of civilization in both East and West which have had a lasting influence right up to our own days. This is a very important and well-known fact which confronts us as a challenge and will continue to do so to the end of time. Many of the great saints and doctors bear witness to it. On the other hand, we must never forget the repeated instances in history when this encounter between cultures and the church has been translated purely and simply into the imposition of a civilization on a people to whom, rather, the good news should have been proclaimed. That is something which must be avoided at all costs. The identification of the gospel with a race, a culture, can result in quite catastrophic situations on a number of levels: ecclesial, cultural, political and social. When that happens, the church's way and its mission is not illuminated by the transfiguring light of Tabor, but by the burning fires of hell, consuming and destroying the work and action of the Holy Spirit.

The Greek Orthodox Patriarchate of Alexandria and all Africa,[1] the origin of which goes back to St Mark the apostle and evangelist, follows and continues the apostolic tradition of the undivided church, which was that of the patriarchate of Alexandria down to the fifth century. After the Fourth Ecumenical Council of Chalcedon in 451 this patriarchate split in two: the one Orthodox, following Chalcedon and the undivided tradition of the church, and the other, with its seat in Cairo in Egypt, following the anti-Chalcedonian Copts.[2] The missionary activity of the Orthodox church took place in the sphere described above. There are plenty of examples of this missionary activity, like the Christianization of Egypt and the creation of a culture, above all in Lower Egypt in the Byzantine period, which made a powerful contribution to the development of the theological thought of the church. In the time of Athanasius the Great it reached as far as Nubia and Abyssinia.[3] The Arab invasion and the establishment of Islam which followed did not allow the continuation of this work.

During the Arab occupation and that of their successors between the eighth and the eighteenth centuries inclusive, although living conditions were very difficult because the patriarchate was considered a loyal supporter of Constantinople, as both a political and an ecclesial power the patriarchate did not cease to engage in pastoral and missionary work among its little flock, providing the parishes with clergy, educating the faithful in the faith, and attempting by collections to raise the necessary money to liberate the Christian slaves who were to be found in the great slave markets of the region. To these immense difficulties one has to add the Catholic proselytism via Uniatism which began after the seventeenth century.

The position looked different after the nineteenth century. The change in the political situation in Egypt, with its autonomy from the Ottoman empire followed by its independence, allowed the reorganization of the flock of Arab and Greek faithful in Egypt and Africa. 1920 saw the first signs of mission from the patriarchate in East Africa under the patriarchate of the great Patriarch Meletios II (1925–1935). This mission was to develop and become organized under the patriarchate of Patriarch Christophorus (1939–1966), which was very important for the church.

Under Patriarch Christophorus three missionary dioceses were established: Irinoupolis (East Africa), Central Africa and Accra (West Africa); the sees of these dioceses were at Nairobi, Kinshasa and Yaoundé respectively. We should note that this missionary movement began with a movement of the Kikuyu tribe to Kenya, towards our church. It would be too long a story to explain why this happened. The second stage was preparation for an indigenous clergy and the organization of parishes. In the time of Patriarch Nicolas VI (1968–86), the seminary Archbishop Makarios III (named after its deceased benefactor) was created in Nairobi for the training of indigenous clergy; this provided preliminary training for candidates for theology and the ministry. They then went on to different theological establishments in the universities of the Orthodox world. Today in East Africa we have one auxiliary African bishop, seventy-nine priests and seven deacons. In Central Africa there are twenty-one priests and seven deacons, and in West Africa twenty-seven priests and two deacons.

Several problems are arising, first the inculturation of the church's tradition in this African context. This is something on which there has been a vast and very complex debate in the church, going back to the Apostolic Council in Jerusalem. This inculturation calls for sustained effort, enormous patience, and boldness in the humility that is in Jesus Christ. What is involved is in effect the continuation of the work of the apostles and the missionaries, including those great enlighteners of the Slavs, Saints Methodius and Cyril. And this activity is taking place in the context of Africa, which rightly calls for justice, and a fight against famine and racial segregation, and has an ardent desire to become a 'new creation'.

Secondly, there is the problem of the financing of this mission; we do not have great resources.

The third problem is the ecumenical training of our faithful and priests. We are not going to start up the old war of religions all over again. We are waiting, praying and working for the unity of the church.

The fourth problem is related to the local traditional religions and Islam.[4]

Nor should we forget – and this is my last point – that some states in Africa and in Asia and the Near East have put restrictions on the life of the church which infringe the fundamental rights of human beings to religious freedom. The Pope of Rome, John Paul II, made a strong and official reference to this, both last year and again this year, in his speech to the Vatican diplomatic corps, when they offered him their good wishes for Christmas and the New Year.

I await with great interest the results of the African Synod convened by His Holiness the Pope of Rome, John Paul II. I offer my prayers for the success of the work accompanying its preparation. Its results may be extremely important for us.

Translated by John Bowden

Notes

1. The Patriarchate ranks second among the local Orthodox Churches after Constantinople, the Ecumenical Patriarchate.

2. The Patriarchate is called 'Greek Orthodox', after the transcription of the Arab and Ottoman term *Rum*, which denoted that its flock were Romans, namely people with the same faith as the inhabitants of new Rome (Constantinople).

3. Abyssinia is present-day Ethiopia.

4. The establishment and reinforcement of Islam in the Christian regions of the Near East is a topic which is vigorously debated.

VI · Bulletins

My Involvement in the Preparatory Work for the African Synod

Bernard Agre

Introduction

The news that an African Synod is soon to be held has burst out like a ray of hope, illuminating the horizon of the young churches of Africa. Millions of believers in God and in Jesus Christ his incarnate Son, millions of men and women of good will, young and adult, have trembled with delight to see the day when Africans will finally express their faith in the true and living God through the logic of their crucified cultures, taking account of the challenges of history.

Perhaps even greater is the emotion of those people who from the beginning have been intimately associated with the preparatory work for this African Synod. And I have the great honour to figure among those taking part in the preparatory work.

My present testimony is in reality a hymn of thanksgiving and hope in the living and merciful God who comes close to us and stamps a new direction and dimension on our journey of faith. It will be in three parts: a historical survey, an expression of my feelings as a participant, and an indication of the challenges to be faced and the questions to be raised.

I Historical survey

The Synod awaited with joy and fervent prayer by the church in Africa, in communion with the universal church, already has a long history. The idea began with the Colloquy which was held at Abidjan in 1977, which ended by expressing the desire that an African Council should soon be held. Here is the text of the resolution:

For Africa to become its own project, for Africans from now on to be their own missionaries, entails a spiritual revolution which affects the present status of Catholicism in Africa and involves its future.

This new situation calls for a serious collective awareness which will include an examination of the function and relevance of the contemporary institutions of Catholicism in its African context. It will compel us to take stock of efforts and experiences which are moving towards Africans taking responsibility for the gospel and themselves, with a view to reorientating the existing authorities and providing mutual instruction. This work of re-evaluation, readjustment and coordination would be stimulated by the perspective of an African Council in which it could culminate.

This Council, which could mobilize the initiative of the African people, would give itself the structures and means needed to put African Catholicity in a state of permanent conciliarity and to help it to assume the task of mission within Africa in all its dimensions – spiritual, intellectual, political and economic.[1]

In fact, at a very early stage there was unease over the idea of a council, not only because of its ill-defined contours, but also because of the difference in opinions to which it led among both theologians and African and Malagasay bishops. Some called for a council and others, more modestly, envisaged a meeting for consultation and reflection at the level of the African churches.

This idea of a council had repercussions on an international scale, among both African theologians who were looking for a 'sounding board' in Europe and elsewhere, and some Westerners who felt called on once again to express their own ideas.

It was in this context of questioning and vagueness, of fears and hesitation, that to general surprise on 6 January 1989, the Feast of the Epiphany, the Holy Father John Paul II announced that an 'African Synod' would be held soon.

After the announcement, he arranged for the formation of a so-called ante-preparatory commission to be formed, to discuss preliminary questions relating to the celebration of the synod. This commission was composed of the presidents of the episcopal conferences of Black Africa, North Africa and of the Church of East Africa. The pope received the commission and defined the subject of the synod as the evangelization of Africa towards the year 2000. The meeting made it possible to identify priorities.

The commission had two working sessions (from 6–8 January and 1–3 March 1989). After this commission had sent its conclusions to the Holy Father, it was enlarged by the addition of nine other members who are not presidents of episcopal conferences, to form the preparatory commission for the synod.

These prelates were to ensure the continuity of the council. The presidents of the regional conferences were to be members only for a limited period while holding office. Several of the first members have already been replaced by their successors.

The council now consists of eighteen members and has been sub-divided into five sub-commissions corresponding to the five sub-themes of the synod: the Proclamation of the Good News of Salvation, Inculturation, Dialogue, Justice and Peace, and Means of Social Communication.

The council met successively in December 1989, June 1990 and lastly September 1990, when it was convened by the Holy Father at Yamoussoukro, on his visit to the Ivory Coast. This meeting can rightly be considered historic, since it was the first to be held on African soil after the announcement of the synod. All the rest were held in Rome. It was during this extraordinary session of the council (between 8 and 10 September), the last part of which was presided over by the Holy Father, that five members designated by the council presented to John Paul II and the public generally the fascicule of the *Lineamenta* (outline), officially promulgated on 9 July at Lome in Togo during the plenary assembly of the Symposium of Episcopal Conferences of Africa and Madagascar (SECAM). Copies of the *Lineamenta*, together with questionnaires, were then sent out for written reactions from all the communities across the continent and the islands. In November 1991 the collective or individual responses will be used by the commission in producing a 'working instrument' (*instrumentum laboris*) which will provide more direct guidance for the debates on the synod due to take place in the middle of 1993. As a member of the ante-preparatory and preparatory commissions I have taken part in the varied preparatory work for the synod with a variety of feelings: pride, uncertainty, and confidence in the Spirit which is the soul of the church.

II Feelings

When called on by the Holy Father to assume such responsibilities, one feels at heart a real pride, the sense of being present at a great opening—proud not for oneself but for the whole church of Africa, which is thus being made the object of so much concern and above all confidence on the part of the Lord. Is this not a way of taking up the challenge made by Pope Paul VI at Kampala in Uganda in 1969, 'Africans, be your own missionaries'?

All the same, beyond this legitimate ecclesial pride there remains a feeling of uncertainty. Ideas flow and jostle together, and in expressing them one asks oneself whether one is not leading the assembly towards unknown horizons. It is at that moment that one becomes aware of the heavy responsibility of participating effectively in debates which must determine the destiny of a large part of the church, and even the whole church. Is this not in a way a reliving of the experience of being on the eve of Vatican II?

At the same time, in the depths of one's heart there arises a reassuring confidence in the Spirit. This Spirit of God, the Spirit of the prologue to the Apocalypse of John, which has spoken to communities in the past (Acts 1.3; 2–3, 1–22), is today seeking to speak to Christians and all those who live, work, struggle, suffer, hope and die in Africa.

Nevertheless, despite the assurance of the Spirit, one is always struck, haunted, by this feeling of security. Will one be able to translate and communicate to the assembly the true aspirations of Africa? I have never prayed so much not to betray the impulses of the Spirit and the expectations of so many churches, which differ so much in views about their futures and yet are at one in their concern for change.

So, having taken part in the preparatory work, I feel assailed by a multitude of questions which are being asked around me about this synod. They might be considered as real challenges which have to be taken up.

III Challenges

The African synod has been announced, and the Christians of Africa are preparing for it with faith, fervour and responsibility. However, some crucial questions arise.

First of all there is the tension created between the ideas of council and synod, a tension which has been 'short-circuited' or resolved by the decision of the Holy Father to convene a 'Special Assembly of the Synod of Bishops on Evangelization in Africa. "You will be my witnesses"'.

This theme makes some people feel really uncomfortable because it gives no precise indication of its intention. It is a kind of trap, or an attempt to content everyone without satisfying anyone.

To many people the adjective 'special' seems suspect.

A second tension arises when one considers the multiplicity of questions to be covered. Can a synod deal with so many questions at once? Since there are too many sub-themes, five in all, is there not a risk of superficiality? Is there really time to examine thoroughly and attentively all these questions, with their delicate and complex contours?

A third tension appearing on the horizon is the possibility of outside influence. Will not this synod be influenced by Rome, the curia and its administrative apparatus, teleprompted by the Holy See, which may declare tabu subjects which are of burning interest to the African continent?

A fourth tension is the question of who will speak for Africa at this synod. Will Africa be able to stand up and say courageously, without useless timidity, what it feels, what it wants to be, in the name of its faith in Jesus Christ? Will it be able to define its 'church status' over against the rest of

Christianity? Could one obtain for all Christianities, or part, this special status in which certain Eastern African and European churches take pride? Africans are now beginning to speak out in a series of studies on the different aspects of the central theme of the synod. The more thorough the preparation, the more opportunities they will have. This is already the place to stress the essential points, convictions and attitudes of the base communities and those at the top.

A fifth tension is caused by the thorny problem of the financing of this synod. The whole of Africa and Madagascar is being approached. Who will pay for this continental convention? Is there not a risk that those monetary forces which would generously like to finance the assembly will make it their instrument? And is not Europe, with its swarm of theologians and technicians, going to impose its own ideas and tell Africa what it does not want, while at the same time hiding the essential points that Africa would like to see emerging? The one who pays the piper often calls the tune. And poverty prevents people from being eloquent.

A sixth point of tension arises over the place where this synod is to be held. Everyone would like the synod to be held in Africa. And the places which have been suggested meet the criteria stated by the preparatory commission for the synod: relative peace in the country, a sizeable Christian population, the possibility of easy communication with the outside world, adequate structures of accommodation to create the best working conditions. The names which keep coming up in this connection are Yamoussokro on the Ivory Coast, Nairobi in Kenya and Kinshasa in Zaire.

The presence of the Holy Father is keenly desired. But will it be the occasion for tranquil truth or respectful and frustrating inhibitions?

These tensions, these questions, are real challenges which must be taken up with courage and faith, and be the occasion for mature consideration rather than sterile polemic. On them depends not only the future of the churches in Africa but also the future of the whole church.

Translated by John Bowden

Notes

1. An extract from the Acts of the Abidjan Colloquy, 12–17 September 1967, under the presidency of M. Alioune Diop, Secretary General of the African Cultural Society, Paris 1978, 371.

African Christianity in European Public Opinion

Rik de Gendt

Africa is dying. At the beginning of last year, when it was estimated that twenty-seven million Africans were threatened with famine and death, and all kind of international organizations were crying out for emergency aid, a massive campaign for solidarity was launched in Belgium under this slogan. The result was strikingly and quite unexpectedly poor; what was raised amounted to barely five per cent of the weekly spendings on a popular lottery. This time, terrible pictures on television of emaciated men, women with dried-out breasts and tens of thousands of dying children with swollen bellies did not have the success hoped for by the organizers. Elsewhere, too, in Europe and in what is called the rich North, public opinion largely remained indifferent to the umpteenth new African drama. Even the simple calculation that the cost of one day of the Gulf War was equivalent to five months' food aid for twenty million Africans threatened by famine made no difference. As far as Europe was concerned, Africa could quietly go on dying. Beyond doubt this realization was a particularly painful one. But that was not all. Not only was there the threat that Africa could perish of drought and civil war; at the same time, the average Western man or woman had lost all interest in it, even in its dying.

The only thing worth a small mention in our press was last year, when one of around twenty local armed conflicts flared up and there was a massive death toll. However, this was only noted in passing. Thus barely had the change of power come about in Addis Ababa, openly supported by the West and warmly welcomed, than the media curtain inexorably came down again on the millions of starving people and refugees elsewhere in Ethiopia. And in the meantime, for months virtually nothing had been said about moribund Liberia or about Mozambique, slowly bleeding to death.

Even the gripping and far-reaching political developments accompanying the difficult course towards a distinctive form of democracy through which the multi-party system is becoming the attraction *par excellence* certainly did not get the attention they deserved in the Western press. Nevertheless, this movement was so extensive that virtually no régime could escape it or feel safe from it. In January 1991 the French Minister for Overseas Development, Jacques Pelletier, could say that of the twenty-nine African countries which traditionally reckoned Paris to be their 'zone of influence', at most five had yet to make a start on democratization. And six months later there were only two: Djibouti and the Seychelles. The English-speaking African countries are not moving ahead so fast, perhaps because London is traditionally less directly concerned than Paris with the internal political affairs of its former colonies, but there too the wind of democracy is blowing strongly.

Overcoming misunderstanding

In the context of these exciting shifts in power, Jan van Cauwelaert,[1] former bishop of Inongo in Zaire and now deeply involved in the peace movement Pax Christi, argued that we 'should overcome our misunderstanding of Africa'. First of all, we need once and for all to get rid of the all too cheap and easy generalizations based only on limited experience, more often than not an experience of disappointment. Moreover, as well as stubborn prejudice and smooth generalizations there is an incredible amount of ignorance about the elementary facts of history and the current situation.

For many people in the West, the history of Africa begins only with the chance discoveries made by the Portuguese sailors who were in fact looking for a sea passage to India and the Far East, or even later, in the nineteenth century, with the great explorations into the African interior. But by that time Black Africa had already had a long history, going back centuries. The material which Africans have handed down orally from generation to generation, their cosmogonies, fables and wisdom sayings, are at the foundation of their civilization. 'Acquaintance with these cultures, a knowledge of the history of Africa and the causes of the decline of a good deal of this impressive African development, can cure us of a great many prejudices about the inability of Blacks to achieve development and can help us to work together in mutual respect.'

So the average European is at least asked to have a positive attitude and an active concern to become well informed about the situation in Africa. If Europeans have no professional concern with Africa, in most cases they will have to refer to specialized journals or other appropriate sources of information. That is usually more than worth the trouble, since particular developments can prove surprising and extremely interesting, and can even provide some useful inspiration and some concrete models for developments on the Europeans' own continent.

Former mission countries

The life of the local Christian churches in Black Africa today largely, though to a lesser degree than political life, meets with this almost universal indifference and ignorance on the part of the rich and developed North. Yet it was precisely this attractive and promising Black continent that in the last century had been the mission territory *par excellence* for the European colonial powers and which had attracted so many youthful forces. Various religious congregations were even established with the almost exclusive aim of the evangelization of Africa. Thus unavoidably and unmistakably, historical and emotional ties developed, also and perhaps even above all in the church sphere, and these continue to remain an integral element of our perception of Africa, though their significance is by no means clear and now they are sometimes regarded as an advantage and sometimes as a burden.

Where some interest has still been shown in the ups and downs of African Christianity, this has been primarily in the former colonies and protectorates. That is all the more understandable since in them there is often still a group of aging missionaries, alongside younger development workers. Moreover the substantial material and financial contributions made by their well-to-do sponsors in Europe are often a by no means insignificant tie. But that, too, is gradually changing. Whereas earlier the money collected was largely, if not almost exclusively, given to the African churches through foreign missionaries, the fund-raising organizations in the North are now increasingly dealing directly with local indigenous church leaders and those in charge of projects, and they even delegate a good deal of the decision-making. This change of course, which puts the emphasis above all on partnership and a mutual trust which cannot always be taken for granted, is also to some degree influencing the European view of circumstances over there. We look at what is happening in the African churches less and less through the eyes of missionaries. We are now learning above all through reports from and contacts with indigenous figures, and these give us a sometimes surprisingly new and refreshing picture of church life there.

Young churches

Along with the decline in the number of missionaries and others from Europe, in the perception of Europeans the old picture of the mission church of Africa has almost automatically had to give way to that of a young church which in many countries has been able to attract and incorporate large numbers of the population. At the same time there is a realization that the attractiveness of the Good News has not always been the chief and decisive reason for this influx, and that Christianity does not always have very deep roots in the life of the people.

According to recent information from AIMIS (Agence d'Informations Missionaires, Rome, October 1990), the Catholic church in Africa numbers 81,883,000 faithful out of a total population of 610,797,000, or 13.4%. Taking the overall growth of the world population into account, Africa is the only continent on which the Catholic church is at present still making evident progress. More generally, the total number of Christians in Africa is put at around 30% of the population. However, the percentages vary considerably from country to country. Everywhere, though, the leadership of the faith communities has largely come into African hands. Thus of 487 Catholic bishops, 369 are indigenous.

What is perhaps looked on in the church circles of the old Europe with some nostalgia – I would almost say 'envy' – is the large number of young enthusiastic believers and the increasing number of vocations to the priesthood and the religious life which dominate the picture of the African church.

Assuming its own forms

The large number and youth of their believers are not the only things we know about the young African churches. Here we also find faith communities which, sometimes compelled by circumstances but often out of deliberate conviction and choice, have developed their own adventurous forms of organization and life. In particular, one thinks automatically of the importance of the base communities, of the significant and serious responsibility of the laity, and of the liturgical celebrations which sweep one off one's feet.

We are sometimes surprised to hear talk from Africa of a parish or a diocese 'as big as Belgium'. In fact the African church is used to a different scale from ours. Parishes as units are often too big and so are divided up into smaller 'base communities'. Although in content these base communities are very different from those in Latin America, the very term 'base community' has a particular attraction for committed believers and therefore arouses their curiosity. European Christians want to know more, above all about the various tasks and the real responsibility entrusted as a matter of course to laity like the mamans catechists or the mokambi.

The element of African Christianity which perhaps makes the most impact on us and has become well known is its distinctive forms of liturgical celebrations. For example, we still find it difficult to envisage a European colleague of the South African Archbishop Desmond Tutu joining in by clapping his hands exuberantly in a church service and dancing joyfully through his cathedral. But we can see above all through closer acquaintance with the Zairean rite of celebrating the eucharist that giving a distinctive form to worship in Africa goes beyond adopting a number of typical African cultural elements, and is also built on distinctive theological and pastoral insights. In Zaire, for example, there is no confession of sins at the beginning of the celebration, as elsewhere in the Roman rite, but it follows the reading of the gospel, the homily and the creed. At that point the priest invites everyone to examine their lives in the light of the message of the gospel and to be converted. In a moment of silence believers bow their heads. Meanwhile the priest goes round the church and sprinkles those present liberally with holy water. This liturgy of penitence and reconciliation is then concluded with a sincere prayer for peace. Above all the authenticity of such an African celebration, the time which is usually devoted to it, the involvement and participation of all present, and the atmosphere of joy are elements which could inspire our sometimes cold and hastily 'read' Sunday masses.

Another aspect of the distinctive form of Christianity which is probably less well known in Europe is the large number of splinter groups, which are usually termed 'independent churches' or 'Afro-Christian churches'. Their common feature is that they are founded by Africans for Africans and that they are strongly orientated on the figure of Christ. Of course as a result they have few contacts outside the African continent, and are dependent on their own resources for their ongoing existence. At this moment there are at least 7,000 such Afro-Christian churches, and more are being created every day. A recent study by the Dominican Sidbe Sempore from Burkina Faso put their membership over the whole continent at 15 million, and by the year 2000 this figure should rise to 30 million. Most of them develop out of the major Christian churches, and some Christians continue to attend these churches regularly, even after joining an independent church. What these people need most, and what attracts them to their new church communities, is their outspoken African character, with a particular concern for the health of the whole person: there are thus all kinds of healing rites and typical expressions of solidarity. The greatest concentrations of independent churches are to be found in South Africa, Zaire and Kenya. The best known is doubtless the Kimbanguist church in Zaire. It was founded by Simon Kimbangu (1889–1951), today has about 3 million members, and was the first Afro-Christian church to be admitted to the World Council of Churches. The phenomenon of these Afro-Christian churches is a real challenge, primarily to the older Catholic and Protestant churches, and so it deserves more attention than it gets at present.

What the church leaders are saying

In his analysis of the involvement of the African churches in the process of democratization, Walter Aelvoet,[2] Director of the *Africa News Bulletin – Bulletin d'Information Africain*, rightly points out that in Europe 'we were accustomed to say that the churches of Latin America were deeply concerned with the "liberation" of oppressed, marginalized people; that the churches of Asia were primarily engaged in "dialogue" with the great religions of the East – Islam, Buddhism, Hinduism, Shintoism, etc.; that the churches of Africa were almost exclusively concerned with "inculturation", specifically with African theology, African liturgy, African catechesis . . . and that they were really less concerned about human rights, justice and peace, freedom, democracy and the wretched material conditions in which human beings have to live.'

From Europe it seemed as though only in South Africa was the church concerned with the contextualization of the message in a setting of oppression and exploitation. Otherwise the African church was above all engaged in building up its own structures, safeguarding its own rights, including freedom for its own sacramental practice and proclamation of the gospel – in short there was a really spiritualistic view of its mission, in a world of poverty and lack of freedom.

This stereotyped European view has suddenly been given a severe shock with the process of democratization that has come about in Africa over the last year. To our surprise, we see that the churches seem not only to be fully occupied with questions of justice, but often are even taking the lead. As Walter Aelvoet continues: 'It is encouraging to note that in many countries the democratic movements are coming to church people with a request for their help over the difficult and very delicate transitional period, simply because these people ultimately seem to have the greatest moral authority; because they had most transcended their own ethnic ties to think in truly nationalist terms; because in thirty years of independence they had shown that they could govern their own communities successfully, whereas the state apparatus had often fallen apart completely, regardless of whether it was capitalist or Marxist. I had not expected this shift. I am more than delighted about it.' In this context one can talk of an African 'liberation theology'.

In contrast to Latin America, in Africa the political commitment which church life has taken on comes less from the base groups than from the hierarchy, and is shaped more by local priests and bishops. Often the African churches are significant enough for most of their leaders not to hesitate openly to express their criticism of the régime in power. There is no doubt that in a great many countries the church is the only structure which has not been fatally tainted with corruption and which can stand up to the existing dictatorships.

This role for bishops and church authorities often seems very unusual to public opinion, where history has been the death of any involvement of the church in political affairs; today, least of all can one imagine a Western European country being governed by a church leader in a crisis. Precisely because they are so unusual, instances of church involvement in African politics are being mentioned in our media. Here I am thinking chiefly of the changes taking place in Benin, Congo and Zaire.

Benin, a country with a Marxist-Leninist régime where Catholics make up a quarter of the population, was first in this respect at the end of 1989, when the bishops suddenly broke their silence in a pastoral letter, 'Be Converted and Benin will live'. Subsequently an appeal was made to the auxiliary bishop of Cotonou, Mgr Isidore de Souza, first to lead the National Conference and then, in the absence of authentic presidential elections, to preside over the Supreme Council of the Republic. For a year – between 19 February 1990 and 4 April 1991 – Bishop de Souza was *de facto* head of his country and was able to lead it towards the beginning of democracy in a peaceful and bloodless way which above all met with general approval.

A second country which is of interest to Europe because of its 'church government' is Congo-Brazzaville, which for twenty years also had a strongly Marxist-Leninist government. When multi-party government was announced there in 1990, there too the bishops produced a balanced pastoral letter: 'Political Commitment, Non-Violence, Brotherhood'. Aware of their own task and the church's responsibility, in it they specifically asked that in the formation of new parties, no party should bear the name Catholic. And when the National Conference began in March 1991, they wrote a new letter: 'Exhortation to Prayer for National Reconstruction'. This time, too, their intervention was simply a service to the country and the people. Moreover they pointed out that 'our churches and chapels must not be turned into a political forum'. Just as in Benin, in Congo the leadership of the National Conference and subsequently of the Supreme Council was entrusted to a bishop, Mgr Ernest N'Kombo of Owando.

According to Walter Aelvoet, 'the best episcopal letters of the historic year 1990 are still perhaps those of the Zairean episcopate'. The memorandum which they sent to President Mobutu on 9 March 1990 in the context of a general referendum was noted all over the world and has become a model for other episcopates confronted with similar problems. The Zairean bishops continue to react to the political and social developments in their country with new letters, 'All Called to Build Up the

Nation', of 16 June; 'Freed from All Fear in the Service of the Nation', of 22 September; 'To Free Democracy', of 23 February 1991; and a 'Declaration to Catholics and People of Good Will in connection with the National Conference', of 21 June. Aelvoet says that it is no coincidence that the Zairean episcopate in this way sometimes had to return to the need for fundamental change, using strong words: 'Their opponent is the most skilful, the most two-faced, the shrewdest and the most ruthless president in all Africa.'

Africa is alive

To judge from what the great Euorpean media say about Africa, the Black continent is at some points as good as dead. Only exceptional events still get some attention now and then. But anyone who pays more specialized attention must concede that Africa is more than ever alive and is worth our attention.

Translated by John Bowden

Notes

1. Jan van Cauwelaert, 'Africa, het miskende continent', *Pax Christi Koerier*, Antwerp, March–April 1991, 2–6.
2. Walter Aelvoet, 'De kerken in het demokratisieringsproces', *Noord Zuid Cahier*, *Wereldwijd Antwerpen*, June 1991, 25–30.

The African Synod: Prolegomena for an African Council?

Engelbert Mveng

Introduction

The Ecumenical Association of African Theologians (EAAT) organized two consultations on the theme of an African Council. In this article I propose to sum up the essence of these two consultations.

The project for an African Council met with an encouraging response among the African intellectuals, then among the theologians, a large part of the African episcopate, and even with the Holy Father, which led to positive expectations. This explains the enthusiasm and optimism of the African theologians. The Symposium of Episcopal Conferences of African and Madagascar (SECAM) set up a theological committee (COMITHEOL) and asked it to provide matter to reflect on with a view to the possible preparation of this event. EAAT moblized its Catholic members, and they organized the two consultations at Yaoundé and Kinshasa.

Certainly the theologians underestimated the difficulties and the obstacles which barred the way to an African Council. So in the last part of this account, I shall try to emphasize these obstacles and to show how, while the talk was originally of an African Council, what has finally come about is an African Synod. But what is the role of this Synod in the growth of the church in Africa? I think that it can mark a decisive step towards an African Council.

I The Yaoundé Consultation (11–12 April 1984)

A consultation was held on 11–12 April 1984 between Catholic theologians, organized by EAAT. Fifteen African theologians, from Zaire, Cameroon, Nigeria, Ghana, Benin, and the Ivory Coast, took part in it, under the presidency of Mgr Tshibangu, Auxiliary Bishop of Kinshasa.

A. *A short history*

The participants heard a report by Fr E. Mveng on the origin and development of the idea of an African Council; other members present added points of detail.

The following stages can be noted:

1. In 1956 the symposium *Questions asked by Black Priests* appeared (in French).

2. In 1962–63, (*a*) a motion passed by Catholic students at their seventh Congress, held in Fribourg from 13–17 April 1962, called for an African episcopal assembly to be held; (*b*) the Society for African Culture (SAC), through two committed laity, Alioune Diop and Georges Ngango, expressed a desire to Pope Paul VI for African participation in the Second Vatican Council and made suggestions about the future of the church in Africa after the Council; (*c*) In 1963 there appeared the volume of essays *African Personality and Catholicism*, published under the aegis of SAC (again in French), expressing aspirations for an authentically African Christianity.

3. Vatican II produced the notion of particular churches and defined the process of their growth to maturity. At Lyons, in December 1982, Cardinal Gantin stated that an African Council had already been spoken of in the corridors of Vatican II.

4. October 1974 saw an official declaration by the African bishops present at the Synod of Bishops in Rome on promoting evangelization in shared responsibility and replacing the theology of adaptation with the theology of incarnation.

5. In September 1977 there was a colloquy at Abidjan under the aegis of SAC on the theme 'Black Civilization and the Catholic Church'. A resolution calling for an African Council was explicitly and publicly passed.[1]

6. In 1981, three African theologians paid a visit to Europe. Again under the aegis of SAC, Abbé Bimwenyi, Secretary-General of the Episcopal Conference of Zaire, and Frs Hebga and Ossama SJ, gave a series of lectures in Paris, Lyons, Brussels and Louvain between 22 November and 4 December to explain the project for the African Council. During their stay they received a telegram of encouragement and support from Cardinal Zoungrana, President of SECAM.

7. SECAM examined the project, and Cardinal Zoungrana, at the suggestion of the Standing Committee of SECAM, charged its Secretary-General with creating a working party to make an in-depth analysis and express its view on the opportunity for an African Council.

8. EAAT, founded at Accra in December 1977, identified itself with the wish for an African Council and included this in its major study projects in 1980.

9. On 3 May 1980, the episcopate of Zaire expressed the desire for an African Council to John Paul II on his visit to Kinshasa.

10. On 12 April 1983, Cardinal Malula, in the name of the episcopate of Zaire, repeated to the pope the same desire for an African Council, 'which would allow our churches to take stock of the present situation of Christianity and to establish in consultation an adequate basis for the integral evangelization of our continent in the future'.

11. On 23 April 1983, in his reply to the second group of bishops from Zaire, in Rome, Pope John Paul II expressed his agreement in principle to the project for an African Council. He added: 'Besides, I have already spoken of the vital need for consultation between all the bishops of Zaire; moreover, I think that to respond to a desire which you have expressed about the whole African church, a consultation is also necessary at this level in one form or another, to examine the religious problems facing the whole of the continent, obviously in liaison with the universal church and the Holy See. But that would leave intact the responsibility of each bishop in his diocese.'

12. In October 1983, the African bishops present at the synod in Rome examined the project for an African Council under the presidency of Cardinal Zoungrana of SECAM and opted for the formula 'African Council' in place of 'African Synod'.

13. A COMITHEOL document dated 2 November 1983 was sent to all the episcopal conferences of Africa and Madagascar on the project for an African Council. This document stated: 'EAAT was one of the bodies, along with SECAM, which seized on the idea and the desire for an African Council expressed by the Abidjan Colloquy in 1977.'

14. On 11–12 April 1984 came the EAAT consultation. Catholic theologians, members of EAAT, studied the project for an African Council in order to submit the fruit of their reflections to the President of SECAM. The SECAM Secretary-General, Fr Joseph Ossei, and Mgrs Monsengwo and Ntedika, President and Secretary-General respectively of COMITHEOL, had indicated their intention of coming but were unable to because of the political situation in Cameroon. In the event, COMITHEOL was represented by His Excellency Mgr Sarpong, President of EAAT and a member of COMITHEOL.

It emerges from this historical sketch that the project for an African Council is a fully ecclesial project and is of the utmost interest to the Catholic theologians who are members of EAAT.

B. Definition and nature

In conformity with canon 439.1, this is a particular regional council, at the level of Africa. The canon speaks directly of a particular plenary council bringing together the particular churches of an episcopal conference. In this case the council is sought at the continental level, and it will bring together all the particular churches which are part of SECAM.

> *Canon 439.1*: 'A plenary council, that is, one which is held for all the particular churches belonging to the same conference of bishops, is to be celebrated as often as it seems necessary to the conference of bishops, with the approval of the Apostolic See.'

In accordance with the arrangements, the African Council will be convened at the level of SECAM by its president, but the prior approval of the Holy See is required.

C. The participants

With reference to canons 439–46, taking account of the necessary characteristics of a particular council at a regional level, the council will bring together:

(*a*) Above all the bishops, who will be joined by representatives of all the people of God in Africa, i.e. priests, religious and duly chosen laity.

(*b*) Foreign missionaries working in Africa, other than bishops (who participate in their own right), who will be invited to the degree that they have positive contributions to make.

In a special category, SECAM could invite a delegation or representation from the Holy See but this would have no voting rights. As observers, SECAM could invite the categories which were represented at Vatican II, namely ecumenical representatives from Africa and even from outside the continent, and from other episcopal conferences.

D. Major problems

The basic proposal is to take stock of the present state of Christianity in Africa, to create conditions for the development of the Christian religion so that it can put down deep roots, and to make a general survey of the present religious situation in Africa.

Ways forward for Christianity in the future will be explored and examined in the following sectors: theology and the doctrinal situation, liturgy, spirituality, overall pastoral orientations and options, and the activity of the church in African society.

E. Suggestions and clarifications

1. A preamble should be produced on the historical and theological foundations of the African Council.

2. Since this is a Catholic project, the Catholic members of EAAT are involved, and are ready to make their specific contribution to the preparation and holding of the African Council. At present they are

working under the aegis of the highest authorities in SECAM and in communion with them.

3. Those taking part in the Yaoundé consultation recommend:

(a) The setting up, in the shortest possible time, of three preparatory technical committees: Anglophone, Francophone and Luso-Hispano-phone.

(b) The setting up of a central technical co-ordinating committee.

(c) The designation of a technical committee to see to the material infrastructure and finance, to be responsible for estimating the cost of the preparations and holding the sessions, and examining sources of finance inside and outside Africa.

4. The members of the Yaoundé consultation would like a list of specific problems needing to be dealt with to be made by the central commission, after consultation with all the people of God in Africa. It is important to stimulate work and research at every level: parishes, Christian communities, major seminaries, faculties of theology, research centres, associations, etc.

Each of these commissions will include specialized sub-commissions on the general situation of Africa, pastoral questions, doctrinal questions, the responsibility and mission of the church in contemporary African society, law, and church discipline.

5. To ensure the full success of the council it is necessary to conscientize and mobilize the whole of the African episcopate. Those taking part in the consultation resolved to send a letter to Cardinal Zoungrana, President of SECAM, and Mgr Sapong, President and Secretary-General of EAAT, and Fr Mveng was instructed to take this letter to the President of SECAM.

6. The consultation recommended that the whole church in Africa should devote itself to prayer for the full success of the African Council.

II The Kinshasa Consultation (23 February 1986)

The second consultation for the project of an African Council was held at Kinshasa, Zaire, on 23 February 1986. Fifteen African theologians from Zaire, Cameroon, Ruanda, Burundi, Nigeria and Ghana took part, under the presidency of Mgr Tshibangu, auxiliary bishop of Kinshasa and founder member of EAAT. On the agenda was:

1. What is the state of the project for an African Council after the Yaoundé consultation?

2. The present situation and the procedure to be followed.

3. Any other business.

1. The state of the project

The participants heard a brief report from Fr E. Mveng, Secretary General of EAAT, on current preparations. There was then a discussion about initiating action, steps to be taken and organizational problems.

The report on current preparations summed up the work of the two theological commissions concerned with the project for a council, COMITHEOL and the Catholic group of EAAT.

So far, COMITHEOL had produced two documents.

A. *African Council*, dated Rome, 2 November 1983, and an appendix entitled 'The Contribution of Particular Councils'. The first document contained elements of replies to six questions, relating to: particular churches and particular councils; the frequency of particular councils; the occasions of particular councils; subjects treated in these councils; the convocation of these councils; influence on the universal church.

B. On the occasion of the Plenary Assembly of SECAM at Kinshasa in July 1984, COMITHEOL produced three documents: *Why an African Council?* (Kinshasa, 9 July 1984), *The History and Activities of COMITHEOL* (Kinshasa, 9 July 1984), and *An African Council* (Kinshasa, 11 July 1984).

C. The Catholic group of EAAT in turn organized a consultation on the African Council at Yaoundé on 11–12 April 1984. Two bishops, a cardinal and twelve theologians, from different regions of Africa, took part. The minutes were submitted first to the standing committee of SECAM in Accra (8 May 1984), and then to the plenary assembly of SECAM in Kinshasa (July 1984). The delegation of Catholic theologians to the standing committee of SECAM consisted of Mgr P. K. Sarpong, Bishop of Kumasi (Ghana), President of EAAT and a member of COMITHEOL; Fr Englebert Mveng, SJ, Secretary General of EAAT; and Abbé Ngindu Mushete, Academic Secretary of the Faculty of Catholic Theology of Kinshasa and a member of the executive committee of EAAT. The delegation of the theologians at Kinshasa consisted of Abbé Ngindu Mushete and Fr Engelbert Mveng, SJ. The latter presented to the SECAM assembly a document entitled *African Council: Historical and Theological Foundations*.

All these documents surveyed all the historical, pastoral and theological questions relating to the possibility of an African Council. The themes to be covered were touched on in the documents of COMITHEOL and EAAT without going into detail. Suggestions were made about the organization and preparation of such an event. At present, one can say that the phase of the theoretical examination of the project of an African Council is drawing to a close. A new stage has to be envisaged, a move towards action.

2. A move towards action

A. This involves several stages. The first is that of ecclesial consultation, providing information for Christian people, sensitizing and mobilizing them. The fact that his Holiness Pope John Paul II mentioned an African 'Council' on his last journey to Africa shows that the work done so far has been brought to his attention and that moreover he sympathizes with it. That is the supreme encouragement for African Catholics.

In keeping with this need for consultation, since 1984 two surveys have been arranged among the African episcopate. The first questionnaire was sent to the African episcopal conferences by SECAM. The second was sent to every African bishop by the Sacred Congregation for the Evangelization of the Peoples. Since the result of these surveys has not been made public, it is not for me to give an account of them here.

The visit of Pope John Paul II to Africa in August 1985 marks an important stage in the developments in Africa and the project of an African Council. Speaking to African intellectuals in Yaoundé on 13 August 1985, among the African church authorities he mentioned the episcopal conferences, SECAM and the Council.

In connection with the second point on the agenda, the following points were considered:

3. Steps being taken

A. Information has not yet been provided for the Christian people of Africa, nor have they yet been sensitized or mobilized. Our consultation should suggest the means and the strategy to be used from now on.

(a) SECAM should immediately produce an information bulletin, to provide a monthly link with all the episcopal conferences and the Holy See. This bulletin would take stock of the real significance of the African Council, its objectives and the stages in its preparation.

(b) The same information should be disseminated widely at the level of episcopal conferences and dioceses, and right down to parish level. The reactions and suggestions of pastors, theologians and faithful should be communicated monthly to the SECAM secretariat.

(c) At the parish level, it should be suggested that bishops call for campaigns of prayer and information. A prayer for the preparations for the council might be suggested to the standing committee of SECAM, to be translated and disseminated throughout the parishes. This prayer could be recited every day, or at least every Sunday in churches and chapels.

(d) At the theological level, as well as the consultations organized by EAAT, SECAM could create a group of experts responsible for organizing seminars to reflect on the regional episcopal conferences.

At this level, the participants stressed the following points:

(a) While they thought this effort to increase awareness was necessary, the theologians felt the need for discretion, to avoid offending the African episcopate by giving the impression of pre-empting or forcing its decisions. Their prime concern was the interest of the churches of Africa in communion with the universal church. For the moment, the important thing was to prepare material which envisaged the actions to be taken as soon as the position of the episcopate was fixed.

In this respect the participants were informed that the survey sent out by SECAM had so far received answers from only eleven out of the thirty-five episcopal conferences contacted, and that the standing committee of SECAM meeting on 24 February 1986 would certainly be concerned with this question.

The participants asked what would happen if the majority of the responses were negative. The unanimous view was that the present work of the theologians should not be thought useless. In every case it was important to continue to make the churches of Africa sensitive to the problems of the people of God in Africa.

Others noted that the pope's position on this project seemed more positive. However, his words had to be put in context: in his speech to the intellectuals of Yaoundé on 13 August 1985, in connection with inculturation the pope had mentioned the 'episcopal conferences, SECAM and the *Council*' among the touchstones for church communion in Africa. This comment was clearly positive.

Other questions were discussed by the participants, in particular:

What purpose was the Council to serve? What would happen after the Council, when Vatican II had yet to be digested? On the other hand, such a council on a continental scale presupposed provincial councils and preparatory synods. There had not been many of them.

The response to this was that the African Council would be a starting point, not a destination. That had also been the case in China and the United States in the previous century.

On the other hand, the Council must be seen as a sharing of experiences between African churches and not the concern of a single church (e.g. that of Zaire). The African Council will in fact be the extension and implementation among us of Vatican II.

Finally, given the extraordinary upsurge in conversions in Africa, the 'African boom', it is necessary for the church in Africa to take stock, to develop strategies for its second evangelization (most of the churches are celebrating their centenary) and to give itself the means of controlling and guiding the 'African boom'. Several African dioceses either have organized or are in process of organizing the synods which ought to be preparing the ground.

In fact, given the absence of information and awareness among the African churches, there is a need to organize regular information at episcopal conferences, and colloquies (for example one on *Ad gentes* and its application).

This process of sensitizing would make it possible to put an end to certain prejudices: thus people would see that the Council, the plan for which was born at Abidjan in 1977, is not a Zairean affair, nor is it even exclusively French-speaking, since English-speaking bishops and theologians have been working on it from the beginning.

On the whole, discussions revolve around two major questions: the justification for an African Council and its aims, and the need to inform, sensitize and inspire the people of God.

In connection with the aims of an African Council, the participants are examining the role of the laity in such an assembly. The very existence of SECAM, a statute for which is being developed, its powers and its programme, could justify the calling of a council. The people of God, by the problems which they pose to us every day, by the very progress of history on our continent, is today the primary partner calling for a council. The churches of Africa cannot face the Africa of the year 2000 in disarray.

The need to inform and sensitize the people of God has led the participants to suggest specific measures, as indicated above: the creation of a SECAM information bulletin, and the organization of special missions.

4. *The procedure to be followed*

The documents of COMITHEOL and EAAT have in practice provided answers from the point of view of tradition and theology to the main questions raised by the project of an African council. It is worth recalling them.

Who convenes such a council? SECAM, after the approval of the Holy See.[2]

What is the nature of such a council? According to canon 439.1 it is a particular plenary council bringing together the particular churches of an episcopal conference. In this case the council is held at the continental level and will bring together all the particular churches which form part of SECAM.[3]

Who takes part? Above all the bishops and representatives of the people of God: priests, religious and duly chosen laity. Then foreign missionaries and special delegates (from the Holy See, without voting rights) and guests (an ecumenical delegation from Africa and even further afield, representatives of other episcopal conferences, etc.).[4]

What would be the date? Consultations so far have not touched directly on this question. The plenary assembly of SECAM at Kinshasa in July 1984 put a good deal of emphasis on the need to devote time to an in-depth preparation for this project. If one takes account of the experience of other plenary councils (those of Baltimore in the USA in the nineteenth century, China [14–28 May 1924], and Indochina [18 November–5 December 1934]), 1990 would be a reasonable date. The immediate preparation of the other plenary councils mentioned above did not take more than a year at most, and communications were less developed than in our day.

The duration. Most of these plenary councils lasted two weeks, though the churches represented were less dispersed than those of the whole of the African continent today. It might be suggested that on the one hand the Council should last a month and on the other hand that it should confer a conciliar status on SECAM which would allow it to prolong the work of the council in its later sessions.

Procedure for convening the Council. As things are, the following steps might be taken. First, SECAM, through its president, refers to the Holy See, submits the whole council dossier to it, and asks for its approval. Secondly, after the approval of the Holy Father, at least the standing committee of SECAM is approached to prepare the convocation. Thirdly, the president of SECAM proceeds to convene the Council.

Before coming to programmes for specific and material organization, the participants asked for two brochures to be produced, one in French and the other in English, containing the texts of all the documents on the project for an African Council developed by COMITHEOL and EAAT. These brochures would be distributed among African bishops, major seminaries, faculties of theology, movement, association and key Christian groups.

5. *Organizational problems*

A. The Yaoundé consultation developed quite a complete plan, but this would need to be filled out and made concrete.[5] A special consultation would probably be needed to achieve this. Meanwhile there was a need to compile a list of the whole African episcopate from the *Pontifical Annuary* and a list of expert theologians by disciplines and by African language zones.

B. The following problems needed to be considered by the commission for finance and material organization.

1. *Host country*: what countries and local churches could host such a council? Suggestions were Kinshasa, Abidjan, Yaoundé, Nairobi, Harare and Ibadan, among others. The question needed to be followed up.

2. *Participants*:

Theologians and representatives	± 400
Special guests	50
Theologians and representatives of the people of God	200

Technicians and others	50
	———
	700

So there should be provision for 1000.

3. There would be the need to plan reception, lodging, food, local transport, secretariat, simultaneous translation, post and telecommunication.

4. *Budget*:

Travel, taking an average of $1500	
per participant (= 1,000 × 1,500)	1,500,000
Lodging (30 × 30 × 1000)	900,000
Secretariat	50,000
Simultaneous translation (4 persons)	24,000
Local transport	50,000
Other	20,000
	———
	2,544,000

This should be rounded up to $3,000,000 = one billion CFA; given inflation this would have to be rounded up further to 1.5 billion CFA.

5. *Sources of finance*. A good deal of this money could be found in Africa itself: from African Christian heads of state if the approaches were made at the highest level; by special collections among the faithful, and from Christian movements (Christian women). It was also possible to count on the Holy See and the generosity of traditional Christian organizations throughout the world.

Recommendations

1. Information and stimulation: noting the absence of any information about this project of an African Council, the participants call on SECAM to create an information bulletin and develop links between the churches of Africa, SECAM and the Holy See.

2. They further propose the organization of sensitizing missions by EAAT, to be led for French-speaking Africa by Fr Mveng and Abbé Ngindu, and for English-speaking Africa by Fr Uzuku, Professor Brookman-Amissah and Fr Mutiso Mbinda.

3. With a view to pursuing their research in a spirit of service and availability, the participants have requested that SECAM should consider their group, which organized the Yaoundé and Kinshasa consultations, to be the group of Catholic consultants from EAAT.

4. Finally, the participants request SECAM and the episcopal conferences to facilitate the launching of a prayer campaign throughout the

continent so that the Spirit of the Lord may be the inspirer and promoter of this African Council.

From the Council to the African Synod

The documents quoted above and those from COMITHEOL claim repeatedly to have surveyed the major problems and to have found an answer to all the questions which stand out as obstacles to an African Council. However, while problems have indeed been identified and other pertinent questions have been asked, it is not true that answers have been found commensurate with the questions.

The first and perhaps most serious problem lies in the African reading of the new *Code of Canon Law*. This reading seems to be unaware of the imprecisions of, not to say the gaps in, this new code. For example, the debate on episcopal conferences and their attributions is far from having been resolved satisfactorily. The doctrine and practice of particular councils, which was so developed in the early churches and which underwent a real renewal in the nineteenth century, seems to have been telescoped in this last code; and the plenary councils, which played such a key role in the mission countries, in the nineteenth century (the Baltimore councils) and the beginning of the twentieth (the plenary councils of China, Japan, Indochina, etc), haveing been reduced to the one level of episcopal conferences, no longer seem to match the whole range of particular national, regional and provincial councils held down the centuries in the churches of East and West.

The ecumenical council itself appears in the new code only as one of the prerogatives of the Sovereign Pontiff, who has the power to convene it, to preside over it and to promulgate its acts.

When the theologians of COMITHEOL and my colleagues of EAAT invoke canons 439–46 of the new *Code of Canon Law*, or when they refer to canon 439.1 to define what an African Council would be, they are putting the cart before the horse. They have not shown in any way how the definition of an episcopal conference given by the *Code* can apply to SECAM. Even those unlettered in canon law, like myself, can see that SECAM does not correspond to any of the ecclesial structures envisaged in the Code of Canon Law. A symposium, in the primary meaning of the word, is a friendly meeting over drinks. Such a gathering has neither statutes nor jurisdiction nor powers. Those who have some acquaintance with SECAM are aware of these gaps.

Even more amazing was the reaction of the great majority of the members of SECAM at Kinshasa in 1984 and later at Lagos when the question was raised of giving SECAM statutes which could have made it an association of episcopal conferences, as happened in Latin America. It was this which made possible the now historical assemblies of Medellin and Puebla.

It is hard to see how SECAM, without legal existence, statutes and powers, could convene a plenary council at a continental level.

Now while this legal void is something that one can only deplore, it is not the result of ignorance or negligence on the part of the members of SECAM. It stems directly from the absence of consensus which divides them. Not only is there no agreement on the significance, function, role and scope of SECAM; there is still division over the opportunities, the content, the programme and the powers of an African Council. The emotional character of some of the debates, emphasizing the disparities between English-speakers and French-speakers, conservatives and progressives, supporters and opponents of inculturation, has quickly led to the identification of scapegoats, first of all among the African theologians, who have been christened 'problem theologians', then in the Zaire episcopate, which has been accused of continental hegemonism, and finally in the person of a man who was an authentic father of the African church, Cardinal Malula, Archbishop of Kinshasa, of holy and blessed memory.

Without doubt the COMITHEOL and EAAT documents take account of the support of African bishops, not to mention the pope, for an African Council. Unfortunately, this support is insufficient in itself to put an end to the differences or to fill the legal void that we deplore. The primary need is incontestably for the African episcopate, at last agreed on the importance of the council, to free SECAM from its aporia by conferring a canonical existence on it, thus providing the conditions for convening a council.

At the very moment when there has been most talk of an African council, one is forced to note that there is no authority in Africa capable of convening such a council. And it is not up to the pope to do this; canon law makes no provisions.

The announcement of an African Synod or, better, a Synod of Bishops on the Evangelization of Africa, can only provoke contradictory reactions. For some it was a final authoritarian stop to the project for an African Council, which was presented in some quarters as a short cut towards an African schism. The most pessimistic proclaimed a real return to fetishism. Some missionaries seized the opportunity to defend their work in Africa against an African church promoted in haste, hardly having emerged from paganism, and always ready to lapse back into it. Others, less pessimistic (and these include the African theologians), see the calling of an 'African Synod' as the quite logical gesture of a pope who, tired of waiting for the African episcopate to take responsibility, has ended by taking it himself, and by doing for the church of Africa what the law allows him to do: to convene a synod of bishops and to designate the evangelization of Africa as a central theme.

Of course, some of the African episcopate have applauded, believing that the pope has purely and simply taken sides with the opponents of an African Council. That is a gross error! Besides, the problems connected with a Synod on Africa belong within the general perspective of the application of Vatican II, which was the very reason for the creation of the synod of bishops. The synod of bishops on Europe, preceding that on Africa, cannot but reassure the most timid and the most hesitant. That having been said, however, the perspective of an African Council is different. It remains open, and totally open. Not only can the next synod not bar the route to it, but again, given the questions and aporias that I have just emphasized, the synod would seem a necessary and salutary step towards the preparation of an African Council.

Though the Synod of Bishops on Europe can reassure some people, an African Synod is a very different matter. There is a great contrast between a Europe which is increasingly unified in political, economic, cultural and religious terms, a Europe in which the Catholic church, present every-where, plays a dynamic and unifying role, and an Africa which is experiencing vast political, economic, cultural and social disintegration, and in which the Catholic church, overwhelmed by an uncontrollable flood of conversions, is trying to cope with people with their backs to the wall – impoverished, starving, without a soul, without a future, without guides and with no reason for hope . . . And at the same time it is being dragged down by the bureaucracy of baptisms to computerize, registers to fill, collections, intentions at mass, and the need to beg alms from overseas benefactors night and day. Such a church is increasingly absent from the places and institutions in which Africa is desperately trying to bring itself together for its own survival: absent from the Organization for African Unity, absent from the Lagos plan, absent from the UNO Economic Commission for Africa, absent from the All Africa Conference of Churches. So our church with its massive numbers seems to be exiling itself on the dramatic periphery of absence, leaving the centre to the mercy of sinful structures which risk stifling it.

The only possible solution in present circumstances would seem to be a synod of bishops on Africa. The hesitations which have surrounded its convocation, the silence which has reigned for more than a year after the announcement of it, the whispers surrounding its preparation, all this has already produced an atmosphere of mistrust, a real malaise compounded by useless clumsiness, in certain Vatican circles betraying practices which are reminiscent of our former oppressors, and which are totally alien to the gospel. There has been much astonished media comment on the names of some members of the preparatory commission. Black lists emanating from Rome are circulating in Africa, suggesting an order to African bishops to remove the famous 'problem theologians', the very ones who are trying to make a humble contribution from Africa to theological research at the end of this twentieth century. How does that look, when one remembers the way in which the bishops, in Europe and elsewhere, choose their expert theologians?

Certainly the African theologians will not be consoled by the reflection that in the long questionnaire circulating in Africa one can find almost everything that has been said by COMITHEOL and the EAAT group. But there are also other spheres where one would have expected the authors of this questionnaire to take account of what has already been said. Unfortunately, however, there is no mention of that.

The first mistake lies in the desire to review everything and say everything at once. The result gives the impression of a superficial, butterfly approach. The first Synod on Africa should begin by identifying the priorities and choosing a limited number of themes from them to go into in depth.

Among the major problems, one is surprised to see so little weight attached to questions such as the missionary effort and the specific contribution of Africa to the evangelization of the world of the twenty-first century. Inculturation is treated with the same haste, not to mention levity. Problems relating to strictly African forms of the consecrated life, to the contextualization of the spiritual life, to the sacralization or the profanation of poverty in Africa, to a legalistic and oppressive ecclesiology in which canon law ignores and stifles the gospel, the transition in Africa from a dependent church to a sharing church – all these problems have been skated over or forgotten in the official preparatory questionnaire. One has the right to ask: what is the ultimate object pursued through the synod? Is it the growth of the church in Africa? Or will the synod stifle it?

One does not seek the growth of the church by denying what the Spirit has brought about in Africa over a century. Who will believe the African cardinal who dares to affirm in public that there are no African theologians? Are there only cardinals, because he is a cardinal? Had he been a theologian, he would doubtless have admitted that there are also theologians. So the church of Jesus Christ has to be tailored to match the fit and colour of our soutanes!

A synod of bishops for Africa has a place in the providential process of the growth of the church on our continent. So it cannot be considered as a parenthesis. It must be prepared for with all the seriousness that such an event merits, and it is a visitation of God in the biblical sense of the word. This visitation is at the same time a questioning and a call to conversion. This conversion is not only that of the infidels. It is above all the conversion of the people of God which is in Africa. The synod will help these people to discover the gap between the call which the Lord is addressing to us and the meanness of our responses. It will reveal to us the reality of an African church which is a free gift from God and which is already there before us, often without us. It will help us to discover, to accept, to assume and to promote this gift of God as the Saviour wants it today and tomorrow for Africa. The synod must help us to discover the African face of the African bride of Christ which is the church on our continent, with all its beauty and its ugliness, with the stigmata of five centuries of oppression, martyrdom, of the anthropological annihilation of Africans on all the continents. It will help us to meet the gaze of our mother the church in Africa, which sounds out our hearts and asks us gravely: 'How long will I have to wait for the day when you achieve in me what is lacking in the Catholic dimension of the body of Christ? Where will you finally make yourself the truly African Catholic church?'

The synod could also help us to recognize the church in Africa, living and present today, with its people of God rich in its immense poverty, with its Christian families, its clergy, its cardinals, its bishops, its priests, its religious, men and women, its thinkers, its theologians, its Christian artists and its spiritual masters. For it is through all these that from now on the church of Jesus Christ will build itself up on our continent, and not with sterile questions about the possibility of an African theology, liturgy or Christian art. They are already there, and since they are already there, they are possible. We do not need useless questions to take us half a century backwards.

That is why the preparation of this synod causes problems. Will this synod sweep the table clean, will it be that of the first harvest? Why is the people of God in Africa ignoring the whole preparation of this synod? For whom, and why, is it being prepared? Why are authentic African theologians being systematically removed? Why are the spiritual masters of our continent being ignored? Why is the impression being given that this is a matter for Vatican officials, in Rome and scattered through Africa, among the ranks of the clergy and in the official institutions. So many embarrassing questions . . .

These questions show that the synod, a divine visitation and call to conversion, will be a decisive step which will allow the church in Africa to discover itself and to become aware of the many challenges which the future poses. By the grace of God this synod can be an opportunity for the church of Africa to discover its conciliar dimension and once again to lay the foundations of a true communion of the churches of Africa to build the kingdom of God on our continent together, in solidarity and charity.

The synod can offer the African episcopate the occasion for giving SECAM a legal structure and a moral persona, like CELAM in Latin America. It is not just in the Vatican that one finds people in high places who deplore the fact that the African churches do not give themselves a sounding board. Why not revive the ancient formula of the patarchiate? Did not Cardinal Lavigerie in the last century bear the honorific title of Primate of All Africa?

Without doubt the way towards titles and honours is one of the greatest obstacles which bar the route to the gathering of the local African churches. An assembly of bishops on the model of the Latin American CELAM would doubtless get a better reception. And such an assembly could then give itself conciliar structures, with periodical sessions. Why not?

If the church of Africa today is not equipped for convening a council, we think, we desire and we pray that the synod of bishops for Africa will constitute a real prolegomena to an authentic, African *Council*.

Translated by John Bowden

Notes

1. See the bulletin *Pour un Concile Africain* 1, Paris 1978.
2. Cf. canons 441–2 and the COMITHEOL document of 2 November 1983, p. 3; cf. also EAAT, Yaoundé consultation, *BTA* 12, 378.
3. Cf. Yaoundé consultation, *BTA* 12, 378.
4. Ibid., 379.
5. Ibid., 380.

Inculturation in the 'Third Church': God's Pentecost or Cultural Revenge?

Metena M'nteba

A. Inculturation: an ecclesial revolution or the return of the same thing?

To judge at least from the frequency of its appearance in bibliographical indexes, the word 'inculturation' has an undeniable and powerful aura for many readers of theological literature over the last three decades. Originally a theoretical concept of missiology,[1] after its use by the Thirty-Second General Congregation of the Jesuits (1974–75) and the 1977 Synod of Bishops, it has also found its way into everyday language, where it is now an accepted term. But whereas a monopoly of usage preserves neologisms from the excesses of fashion and the hollowness of oratory, on popularization they inevitably become much more precise. This inevitably results in a bias in their semantics, not to mention a brake on their original dynamism. The concept of inculturation has not escaped this inflation.

While some people claim that inculturation is an urgent matter and are engaged in formulating criteria for it and planning the stages to be gone through, others are asking whether the enterprise is really new. In spite of the optimistic way in which they are formulated, the questions about inculturation raised by the council responsible for preparing the African Synod express this same perplexity when faced with inculturation: what does this amount to which is new and different from the traditional orthopraxy of the church? Does it usher in an ecclesial 'Copernican revolution' or is it just another example of the return of the same thing in a more or less updated way, an example of what St Augustine called 'Christian solecisms'?[2] The range of answers suggested so far displays two major tendencies.

For some, there is nothing of an 'ecclesial Copernican revolution' about inculturation. The concept simply revives an already known practice of the church which has gained a certain novelty today in the wake of the heightened affirmation of cultural identities and the increased attention of pastors and theologians to anything related to the incarnation of the church in the diversity of cultures.[3]

For others, the concept heralds an unprecedented phenomenon, the turning upside down of the basic actions and traditions of Christianity by new Christianities, and the adoption of them in such a way that Christianity becomes the authentic work and expression of their own evangelization and their nature as church. Thus inculturation denotes a complex process, quite the opposite to a facile indigenization and an imitative reception of Christianity. It implies an action in which the young churches take over Christianity and 'transform the present system of relationships'.[4]

These two theses are in confrontation without refuting each other. In fact they would seem to share a common conviction, namely that inculturation requires a process of cross-cultural negotiation and appropriation of the faith; that it aims at initiating a poetics of faith and diakonia which is lived out and implemented at the interface between identity and action. So both positions, each in its own way, reject any standardization or any a-cultural or a-temporal version of the Christian faith. They thus agree in describing inculturation as a dialectic of the rooting of Christianity in the various cultures of humanity which transforms these cultures at the deepest level by integrating them into Christianity. However, this agreement immediately turns to disagreement once the terms and modes of this dialectic have to be determined.

For some, it is the 'Word of God', or the 'gospel', or even the 'revealed message' which has to 'adapt itself' to or 'naturalize itself' in the different cultures, in the same way as the 'Word made flesh' (the inculturation-incarnation paradigm). Others argue that it is 'Christian faith' which must be 'inculturated' in such a way that, transformed by the leaven of the gospel and regenerated by Christian faith and tradition, through their own cultural genius the host cultures produce an African face of Christianity.[5] This is the 'conversionist' tendency. Yet others favour a 'creative assumption' or a 'critical acceptance' of the original features and actions of Christianity such that the way in which they are expressed among Africans is the authentic product of a synthesis between their existential situation and the power of the message and the resurrection of Christ (the 'inculturation-restatement paradigm). As we shall see, African efforts at inculturation fall into these two patterns.

B. The dominant African paradigms of inculturation

The inculturation movement in Africa is the successor to the theological movement of 'stepping stones' and 'pastorals on indigenization' which followed the council. This decisive turning point has come about under the pressure of nationalist policies orchestrated by the movements for African self-determination which accused Christianity of perpetuating Western imperialism and colonial alienation in Africa under cover of the faith.[6] It is these 'suspicions' which are prompting the African churches to take account of the hope which is in them and to live in a responsible way. In fact, while the charges of the denigrators were always somewhat exaggerated, they did hit on the way in which a number of African Christians have assimilated the tenets and practices of colonial theodicy under the veneer of Christian faith.

1. To be or not to be African, or what is at stake for Christianity in Africa

How can one remain Christian without 'alienating' and denying oneself? This is the crucial question which will dynamize reflection on 'an African style of Christianity'.[7] Moreover, on the eve of the festivities for the first centenary of the evangelization of Black Africa, it can be sub-divided into a number of secondary questions, like the future of Christianity in Africa, or the pastoral policies which are best capable of giving it a chance not only to survive but also to thrive and flourish. These are the questions analysed by E. J. Penoukou in an excellent book, which plays on the twofold aspects of retrospect and prospect. In his view, the inculturation of faith is not only a unique and urgent challenge for the African churches, but also what is at stake if they are to exist and be profoundly African.

> The only serious problem for our African churches is that of the inculturation of the Christian faith. Our churches of Africa will either be African or they will not exist. That is what is really at stake for the future of Christianity among us.[8]

This statement by Penoukou is not a new one. It simply revives a proposal by John XXIII on the eve of Vatican II. But the interesting thing about Penoukou's reflections is the way in which they show the progressive identification made by African Christians between the inculturation of the faith and the work of building up truly African churches, in their soul as well as in civil life. To be integrally African, seen as a horizon and goal of the process, is represented by an ellipse in which the cultural genius of Africa as affected by the political partitions of the continent is one pole and Christianity the other, while the Africanization of Christianity is the major axis.

It is important to take this change into account if we are to understand the two major orientations which will characterize inculturation in Africa: 1. the current of 'inculturation – conversion to Christianity', and 2. that of 'inculturation – African restatement of Christianity'. Both share the conviction that 'from now on there is no room for anyone who wants to regulate African life from outside in the name of an absolute knowledge and a domineering mission'.[9]

2. Inculturation-conversion

This current is rooted in the 'adaptionist' perspective distinctive of Vatican II and Paul VI's encyclical *Evangelii Nuntiandi*. It is illustrated in Africa by Mgr A. T. Sanon. His first book *Tierce-Eglise, ma mère. Conversion d'une communauté paiene au Christ* (1972), like the one written ten years later in collaboration with R. Luneau, *Enraciner l'évangile. Initiation africaine et pédagogie de la foi* (1982), adopt the same approach and aim at the same goal, the development of a pedagogy and a conceptualization of the faith which, taking the African cultural heritage into account, would lead to a harmonious rooting of the gospel and Christianity in Africa.

Mgr Sanon and his disciples put this rooting of the gospel in Africa at the end of a twofold activity, the first stage of which is hermeneutical. It consists in transposing the essential emphases of Christianity into African keys so that they are given an African name and an African face.[10] The second, somewhat cathartic, stage aims at the spiritual and interior purification of African culture under the irradiating effect of 'the light of revelation'. This methodology is based on the thesis that the relationship of Christianity to cultures is not antagonistic; rather, it illuminates and liberates the grace which flows anonymously through all the cultures of humanity. As Mgr Sanon and R. Luneau write:

> We are experimenting how Christianity can come without destroying a culture. It brings cultures a revealing light which shows up their ambiguities and their aberrations. The strongest impression is that of a cultural humanity which has gone for a long time with grace crouching at its feet; and then, all of a sudden, like a gigantic snake, this grace rears up.[11]

Despite its catechetical results, this 'inculturation-conversion' raises a number of questions.

1. First of all, is there any certainty that at the end of the *en-culturation* of Christian symbolism (for this what is going on at the hermeneutical stage of the process) a synthesis will be achieved between Christianity and the cultures concerned? Is it not rather the case that African cultures in

general, like many other cultures in the world, are opposed in one way or another to the gospel and Christianity, by very reason of their riches? If the graft has taken, or can take, so easily in Africa, is it not because, having been destructured, the traditional cultures have become porous to any alien infiltration? And if that is the case, what is the use of the return to (or the detour by) 'ancestralities' which the inculturation-conversion approach recommends? Is it not more important simply to live out the hybrid form of the faith which arises out of the impact of the West on Africa?

2. Is there any certainty that the 'light of revelation' results in the purification of cultures if after two millennia of Christianity the 'Christian-ized' cultures of the East and West do not yet reflect the light of the resurrection, and if their everyday praxis so often infringes the law of Christian love? (If so, how can it be arrived at?) What would be the point of being shown up without a firm intent to be converted? If it is not to be crippling, annoyance at this strongly suggests, indeed compels, a re-definition of terms and objectives.

3. Finally, what is the primordial status of that Christianity which seeks 'local expressions' in order to survive in Africa? If 'the strongest impression is that of a cultural humanity which has gone for a long time with grace crouching at its feet', which suddenly feels its constraining power, does that not suggest that there are not two economies of divine salvation, but just one, achieved by different ways, which though they are different are not alien to each other? And if that is the case, what is the specific character of this Christianity which is said only to shed a 'revealing light' on aberrations and cultural ambiguities? *Mutatis mutandis*, the problem resembles that of inter-religious dialogue in relation to Christian mission. These are serious questions which the conversionist current passes over in silence, though they are inherent in its enterprise.

These questions are not intended to discredit the researches and results of the 'inculturation-conversion' approach. They underline the dangers of accommodation and constructivism inherent in its methodology. What in fact is the epistemological process which authorizes the 'Africanists' to transpose the contents of African customs and institutions into a theolog-ical key which is alien to them? How do they move, within the new theological developments and structures that they obtain, from the traditional to the contemporary and a synthesis of the 'aberrations', 'ambiguities' and the 'revealing light' of Christianity?

Is not this transition achieved only at the cost of a prior reduction of the systemic to the linguistic or by substituting for a fluidity of identity an abolutizing nominalism which freezes Africa and the Africans in mythical entities or in deterministic conceptual concretions? Before being a theoretical and operative concept of anthropology or of ethnology, is not

African initiation, which the adaptationists use as a point of reference, a language, an institution, a social practice, a know-how, with its own codes and symbolism developed with a view to very precise and circumscribed results?

What in fact does initiation teach, and what does the initiated know? 'Nothing', say the initiates themselves, except that the Supreme Knowledge is that there is nothing to know, and that beyond the bursting out of the final laugh there is only the self, the law of the secret, silence and death. This is a very Sibylline statement, the enigmatic character of which should put us on guard against excessive dealings in 'ancestral imagery' or 'Africanisms', the neutralizing or explosive effects of which we do not always measure sufficiently within the syntheses into which our theological alchemies incorporate them.

If it is highly improbable that the precipitations thus obtained are inoffensive to African culture because they are external usages, there are strong reasons for fearing that the chain reactions which they cause are to strong for the sorcerers' apprentices to control, to the great detriment of Christianity. Analyses of the way in which the African separatists took over Christian symbols and actions at the dawn of independence,[12] to turn them against their authors, are highly instructive and would be worth re-reading on the eve of the approaching African Synod.

Cultures are living entities, more or less receptive to the unaccustomed and to novelty, but always self-sufficient and jealous of their integrity. That is the presupposition which one must always keep in mind in any desire to initiate the dialogue between the cultures and Christianity. The outcome of this encounter certainly depends on divine providence, but it also depends on what interests are at stake. To recognize this does not mean putting an end to God's plan. On the contrary, it means taking seriously the death sentence on Christ and the drama of his passion. The same goes for the history of the church: it is a work of the Spirit of Christ, who continues his work in the world and in it achieves all sanctification, but also produces human beings who are simultaneously listening to the Spirit of God, their passions and their interests.

So for Africans what matters is to discover the countenance of God, who, even today, offers human beings his covenant, God in whom they believe, taking account of the histories which they have experienced, their present anthropological and social situation, and their wishes. This involves their formulating and telling themselves what benefit the Christian deity could bring and what benefit being a Christian could be in their conditions, in this world which is theirs. It is this 'appropriation' of the divine which distinguishes the different ways in which the different Christian peoples and groups entered Christianity and explains the advent of the different Christian *leges orandi et credendi* in the history of the church. Why should Christianity in Africa escape this logic of appropriation and get its African countenance from a black and white daub or the artifice of theological plastic surgery?

3. The 'inculturation-restatement' current

This current of thought, already strongly affirmed in the debates and discussions over an African Council, characterizes African theological reflection after the debates on whether or not there is an African philosophy, and on the theologies of indigenization and contextualization. It is expressed most boldly and most systematically in the work of Eboussi Boulaga. The author's main thesis is that Christianity will never be credible in Africa, or at least will suffer a failure to adapt there, as long as it does not allow itself to be 'restated' by Africans in the light of their concrete situation.[13] For Eboussi, this concept of restatement includes the taking over, by Africa, of the 'original' (the memory of Jesus Christ) and the 'foundations' (the inaugural acts of Christianity) by including them in Africa's own schemes and languages.

An article by Eboussi written before the publication of his *Christianisme sans fétiche* enables us to clarify his present proposal. When he speaks of foundations and the original, he means 'that which permanently authorizes Christian experience, its habitual point of reference',[14] i.e. Christ as a 'figure of fulfilled humanity' which can be re-appropriated by all human beings and is valid for any existential situation. The whole work of inculturation lies in this permanent effort of Christians to revive the event of Jesus Christ and to adjust it to their social and cultural context. To be a Christian is not primarily to adhere to a creed, a tradition or a 'way of life'. To be a Christian, for Eboussi, consists in living out the 'Christic model'[15] consistently, and in the authenticity of one's existential situation, and in displaying in one's being the power of the resurrection. It consists in asking oneself how Christianity makes it possible to express the human condition in one's existential situation in such a way as to hold in check selfish and arbitrary forces and to bring about the triumph of the unique commandment of love.

The 'rules of conversion' which follow the exposition of the 'Christic model' are meant, in Eboussi's work, to provide a 'discourse on method' or a *vade mecum* which make it possible to move from contemplation of the Christic model to an effective implementation of it in an African Christian praxis. But although Eboussi's explanation is fascinating, and the power of his 'Christic model' holds the intellectual interest of the reader, his approach cools down the spontaneous enthusiasm of faith and the unconditional adherence to dogmatic statements. Is the Christ of the

Christic model still the 'Word made flesh' of the Gospels and the Jesus Christ of Christian tradition? Is he still God if he is not quite simply God? Can he truly be God if he is 'son of the Mother, son of man, before being Son of the Father or Son of God'?

Is this a denial of the divinity of Christ? What do the grammar and logic of the statement convey? Grammatically, Eboussi's thesis articulates three propositions which are syntactically independent but semiologically linked by a skilful procedure of semantic compenetration which plays on the double register of *implication* and *condensation*, as is shown by the following analysis:

1. Jesus Christ is not just simply God   (P 1)
2. He is   – son of the Mother   (P′2)
                      – son of man
   before being
                      – Son of the Father (P″2)   (P 2)
   or   – Son of God.
3. For us he is the figure of fulfilled humanity (P 3)

The semantic compenetration comes about through the sense of the incompleteness created by the insertion of the adverb 'just simply' in the proposition (P 1) after the negative 'not' and which calls for the affirmative of the proposition (P 2), rather as the centripetal force provokes the centrifugal movement in the dynamic of a mobile. The proposition (P 2) in turn unfolds on the basis of the same logic. It dissociates and then reconciles, by a play with parallelism and homonomy, two concepts which prove to be different by virtue of the typographic artifice of lower and upper case (son/Son). In this dialectical process, the third proposition arises as the synthesis which, while safeguarding the freedoms of (P 1) and (P 2), subsumes them in a superior unity in which their tensions are reconciled without being blurred.

All Eboussi's thought evidently comes into play in the proposition (P 2), which condenses the major thesis of his christology. This proposition (P 2) is structured around five key concepts: Jesus Christ (c_1), son of the Mother (c_2), son of man (c_3), Son of the Father (c_4) and Son of God (c_5) -- Jesus Christ being the subject term around which the four other terms are organized as predicates. These four attributive concepts share a common factor which at the same time binds them together and differentiates them: they are all composed of the same seme (son), which is phonologically identical but morphologically different. The differentiation is achieved by the artifice of lower and upper case (son/Son), by the effect of redundancy (son), and the chiasmus which is evident in the determinative parts of four predicates:

son of the Mother (c 2) <——> son of man (c 3)
Son of the Father (c 4) <——> Son of God (c 5)

These details, which seem insignificant to a reader in a hurry, nevertheless prove important in analysis: the rhythms, the redundancies and the chiasmuses hide a clash. By producing breaks and connections, these stylistic procedures introduce subtle analogies which veil what is explicit in order to make what is hinted at eloquent. This (P 2) is a strange proposition. It comprises two sub-propositions (P'2) and (P''2), linked together by the adverbial locution 'before', which, by marking the priority of the 'being son' to the 'being Son', reinforces the break in perspective started by the typographical artifice of lower and upper case. So, for Eboussi, only the attributes relative to human generation (c 2 and c 3), i.e. the predicates of type (s), are quidditatively applicable to Jesus (JC). Those of type (S) only 'suit' him once the existential priority of the former has been posited.

Would Eboussi be suggesting the priority of the humanity of Christ over his deity? And if that proved to be the case, of what order would this priority be, and, as a corollary, what would be the principle of the coexistence of humanity and divinity in Jesus? Is Jesus' 'being' Son a mode of his being God or the product of a historical or mythological affectation? The dialectic of activity and passivity expressed in this question is enough on its own to identify the issue. It only needs to be faced to see the mode of co-existence which Eboussi is conferring on his two categories of Christian attributes. The difficulty thus moves from the antithesis to the thesis. It is reconcentrated in (P 1), or rather in the adverbial phrase 'quite simply'. 'Jesus is not quite simply God.' (That is the proposition (P 1.) How are we to understand it?

This proposition is susceptible to two contrary interpretations, depending on the function that one assigns to the adverbial locution 'quite simply'. If one links the negative form of the copula to the adverb by transferring this latter to a median position in the auxiliary of the negation, one creates a new grammatical complexion which denies the divinity of Jesus: 'Jesus would not be quite simply God.' If, by contrast, one shifts the modifying impact of the adverb to the attribute of the proposition (God), as Eboussi does, the proposition 'Jesus is not quite simply God' signifies that the predicate (God) 'suits' its subject (Jesus), but in accordance with a modality (or modalities) which is (or are) not simple.

The equivocation certainly remains. Despite its persistence, I incline to the second understanding of Eboussi's proposition because: 1. The first interpretation can be sustained only by altering the author's proposition. This is an alternation which produces a semantic complexion alien to

Eboussi's proposition. 2. Grammatical rules teach us that an adverb modifies either a verb, an adjective, another adverb, a prepositional phrase or an attached subordinate clause. This is a rule which Eboussi clearly observes. What do we conclude from this?

Despite his stress on the need for the existential dimension in any authentic reception of Christianity, Eboussi's Christic model evacuates the divine pre-existence of Christ in the very act of affirming his possible divinity. If not being quite simply God does not denote that one is not God at all, it can denote that one is God by acclamation, decree or power of attorney. So Eboussi's Christ 'who is a figure of fulfilled humanity' becomes problematical for the African who holds to the present creed of the Catholic church, and for 'simple people' an ideal on which even the pragmatism of the 'rules of conversion' could not confer a real humanity, because Eboussi's Christ so much inhabits these regions of reality in which understanding runs alongside history, but does so in accordance with the atemporal process of essences.

In fact Eboussi, who is far too intelligent to fall into adoptionism or Arianism, exiles the Christ into a transcendence which removes him from all domestication and all ideological recycling. The 'auto-christification' of the self through imitation of the 'Christic model' becomes the only respectable way of approaching the divine. In short, each of us can realize the Christ in ourselves and become another Christ in our turn if we stamp the consistency of Christic existence on our everyday appearance. Hence the question: would the true inculturation of faith in Africa by self-determination consist in saying that the African is capable of incarnating God and realizing him? To what degree does this Promethean adventure of self-Christification strictly mean acceding to oneself, not only by freeing oneself from all achievements, but by saving oneself, god by god, step by step, from every God? These are the questions which the paradigm raises.

4. A Christianity which runs counter to dogmas and doctrines?

A Christianity which runs counter to dogmas and doctrines! That is the logical consequence of the thesis analysed above, in which one discovers in filigree the colour in the process of the inculturation of Christianity in the new African and Asian Christianities. The basic question which structures reflection thus works out like this: can one be truly and authentically Christian while continuing to evolve in the institutional, epistemological and aesthetic framework of the West? Is there only one uniform way of doing science, of believing, celebrating, living – in short, being? This question arises out of a life affected by the devaluation of subject cultures and the regaining of subsequent awareness of oneself as a personality who has for long been denied as a person.

In an African Christian setting, this question is expressed clearly for the first time in *Des prêtres noirs s'interrogent* (1956), and becomes more radical in Meinrad Hebga's *Emancipation of Churches in Tutelage*. 'We want Jesus Christ as a unique supreme point of reference.'[16] The author begins from the thesis that Christianity is not a Western but an Eastern religion. However, in the course of history the West has monopolized it and imprinted on it the indelible seal of its philosophy, its law and its culture. That was its most legitimate right. But it is an illegitimate enterprise if today it seeks to impose this cultural and historical package of Christianity on other peoples of the world who have come late to belief in Jesus Christ, as though it were essential to the nucleus of Christianity. Hence, Hebga thinks, the advent of an African Christianity presupposes that Africans are becoming emancipated from the tutelage and the cultural adoption of Christianity by the West, returning to the original Eastern nucleus and stamping on it in turn the indelible seal of their profound Africanness. For Hebga, this work passes through the relativization of the Aristotelian-Thomistic apparatus and through the purging of faith in Jesus Christ from French, Greco-Roman, Lusitanian, Spanish and German usages and customs, 'Christianized' and divinized by Europe.[17]

To sum up, the task is to dissociate faith in Jesus Christ from its Western expression. That poses for the very first time and in all its brutality the problem of the relationship between faith and cultures in Africa. It does so no longer in terms of theology or metaphysics, but quite simply in terms of history. But can one easily dissociate faith in Jesus Christ from its Mediterranean and Western conditioning: Can one happily run counter to dogma and doctrine and return to the Semitic original, appropriate it and update it after two thousand years of history?

When one raises these questions, there are those who retort that this claim can only end up in the paradox of the botanist who peels an onion in the vain hope of extracting the kernel. The objection is not irrefutable, since not all vegetables are of the bulb kind and there is all the difference (an ontological difference) between the onion and the history of Christianity and its doctrinal development, the difference between the growth of a vegetable and that of a body which claims to be mystic. But if the choice of the metaphor of the onion is arbitrary, the image well reflects the way in which Christianity is made up: of successive deposits and superimpositions of layers of traditions, in other words, by a progressive 'inculturation'.

To recognize that Christianity is 'progressively constituted' is to accept its historical and cultural dimensions. In this sense the expression 'faith running counter to dogmas and doctrines' could be understood as a cry of protest from the cultural universes which have for long been kept down and are now deciding to give birth anew to the Word of God through their own experience. Positively, the expression states a refusal, or better a concern, not to grow by proxy or by the interposition of cultural traditions. Is the enterprise a mirage? And if not, how could it be achieved?

C. Towards a happy inculturation of faith

1 . Christianity against culture: a false question?

I agree with Pope John XXIII and E. J. Penoukou that Christianity in Africa will either be African or it will not exist there at all. But this 'Africanness' will not be achieved either by a Christianization of Africa or by an Africanization of Christianity, but by an existential assumption by the African of the gospel of salvation. There is nothing unusual about this thesis if one is prepared to admit that to 'Christianize' Africa can in fact only mean transposing to it a certain form of Christian religion, and conversely that to 'Africanize' this form in fact amounts to making black or tropicalizing a Christianity (or one of the Christianities) which has already been acculturated in other times and other places.

The defect stems from a contrasting of 'Christianity' and 'cultures' as two realities or as distinct spheres of human existence. This opposition itself stems from the thesis that 'Christianity, by its vocation to be universal, does not belong to any culture'. This thesis is built on contrasting clichés like spiritual/temporal, Christian/human, culture/ faith, universal/particular, taken in a strong sense because this makes it easy to construct discourse. These contrasts always engender false alternatives, not because the contrasts are not relevant in themselves but because they are used so exclusively.

What does it really mean to say on the one hand that 'Christianity, by its vocation to be universal, does not belong to any culture', and on the other hand that the Christian is not different from other people, that Christians have to live out their Christianity within the framework of the culture to which they belong? What does this mean, if not that Christianity in itself only exists as a limiting concept, that one only meets it in specific conditions, in a historical state, even if one has to accept that its supra-temporal idea plays, and must play, a necessary and dynamizing regulatory role?

The problem of the relationship between Christianity and culture is certainly posed wrongly or is just an excuse if it is insisted that Christianity is a religion of the Book and related to the ethnic history of Israel, to the incarnation of the Son, to the stages and areas of its development in the Mediterranean and the West. In my view, the real problem is not that of the relationship of the gospel to human culture, but that of the relationship of new Christian traditions to those which have monopolized Christianity hitherto. It is not so much inter-cultural exchange which causes problems as the fact that in the course of the history of Christianity the 'Christianists' have attached to God certain political and cultural options shaped by particular interests.

Exported to or proclaimed in regions which defend other interests or have chosen other cultural options, this God blushes and no longer knows what he wants, so long has he been put, successively or simultaneously, at the apex of hierarchies and régimes, sometimes antagonistic but always diverse and self-interested. To recognize this traffic in the divine is to devalue not the God of Jesus Christ and Christian faith but his historical counterfeits. Inculturation as a concern for a cultural appropriation of the act of believing would today seem to be iconoclastic, since it sets in motion a negotiation and a restructuring of religious capital among agents whose interests and preoccupations diverge.

2. *A possible way out: opening the doors to the Spirit*

The situation of inculturation thus offers only one median way out: that of taking seriously and promoting a catholicity which leaves open to Christian communities the possibility of a different realization of their capacity to integrate 'the common deposit' into their own economy, making sure that there is neither alteration nor fundamental transformation of the essential content of the faith received by the apostles. It is not so much syncretism or heresy which are the problem in this 'different realization of the faith' (as some people fear) as the question 'how can one further the work of inculturation without the *magisterium* on the one hand abdicating its prerogatives and on the other losing any of those whom the Father has entrusted to it, even the son of perdition?'

John Paul II raised this problem for the first time in his address on 30 April 1983 to the bishops of the ecclesiastical provinces of Kananga and Lubumbashi in Zaire,[18] when they were on an *ad limina* visit. The major thesis of this address is that the work of inculturation calls for a combination of theological reflection and ecclesial practice, the rationality of which is marked in both content and method by an ecclesiology of communion and dialogue within the Christian community concerned. The pope is not innovating on this particular point. He is developing the proposals of Paul VI to the members of the International Theological Commission.[19] But will not this happy ecclesiological perspective be limited by the way in which the pope distributes the *munera* between the different members of the people of God: the bishops, theologians and faithful?

In fact, when the pope is specific about the roles or orders of participation of the people of God in the 'long and courageous process' of the inculturation of faith, he assigns only a passive role to Christians who are not theologians and not bishops: they are simply to be instructed, guided towards holiness, and trained for their various ecclesial and social responsibilities.[20] This is a passivity which contrasts with the 'activity' of the *munera* of the theologians, on whom the pope confers the role of formal coadjutors of the *magisterium*, especially in any approach to new questions and in the technical deepening of the sources of faith, and of the bishops, who are designated 'doctors and fathers in the faith' and judges of the last instance, in union with Peter's successor, of the Christian authenticity of ideas and experiences.[21]

One's overall impression is that the faithful are treated here simply as the object of the pastoral concern of the hierarchy or even as a field of experimentation for theologians. The whole enterprise of inculturation is entrusted to people working within the strict limits of the sphere controlled by the authorities, who have both the right to judge and the right to approve. As if hierarchies, by reason of the degree of authority conferred on them, had a kind of prior claim on the grace of God or the inspiration of the Holy Spirit!

As the elaboration and adoption of the faith of the church by the communities, inculturation calls for a pastoral approach which is more attentive and sensitive to the heartbeat of all the people of God and its *sensus fidei* than theological constructions issuing from academic think-tanks. It would be quite wrong to exert strict control over the work of inculturation like states seeking the linguistic or political unification of their territories.

The formidable dilemma which growing Christianity faced at the time of the Council of Jerusalem (Acts 15.1–35) and the incident at Antioch (Gal. 2.1–10) show us the possible results of the encounter of the gospel with other cultures: synthesis or reception involving two different cultural universes can result either in the victory (and accompanying submission) of one universe over the other, in resistance, or in dialogue which respects the ways of the Spirit and the profound authenticity of those who welcome the word of God (Acts 15.13–21). The way in which these two conflicts were resolved bears witness that the inculturation of faith in Jesus Christ involves a dialectical process of encounter between the gospel of Christ and the genius of the culture which experiences from it the power of resurrection and a fertile integrity of being. So the gospel does not adapt itself to cultures, nor do cultures adapt themselves to the gospel. They meet, clash and test each other mutually, like gold and fire in the crucible.

It is this 'encounter – confrontation – test' which brings about the cultural 'new creation' in which the gospel is appropriated as a power of redemption and recreation: 'Behold, I make all things new' (Rev. 21.5). This work is possible only in an ecclesiology of communion which makes the Holy Spirit and the eucharistic mystery the chief of its premises, and in a living Christianity which through lucid discernment makes the past more profound and at the same time opens up the cultures to universal values common to all human beings and to the particular values of other cultures, by surmounting the inevitable tensions and conflict through dialogue and a deeper understanding of origins. Do not let us be afraid! Let us open up the gates to the Spirit of Pentecost and the Redeemer!

3. Three features of an African theology at the service of inculturation

(a) A theology which achieves a healthy 'demythologization'

An African theology which put itself at the service of an African expression of the faith would be a theology which achieved a healthy 'demythologizing' language. The adjective has nothing to do with Bultmann's exegesis in his existentialist interpretation of Christianity. It simply conveys the conviction shared by J. Daniélou and K. Rahner that, despite the permanence of Christian identity, in future the expression of faith will be conceptualized in a different way and establish other connections and perspectives than those of today. This is simply because of the nature of Christian catechesis, which requires the statements of faith to be proclaimed in a way which can be believed and received (= not in a mythological way) by its hearers.[22]

This change in expression does not, therefore, stem from a morbid desire to be different, but from the very demand of 'faith in search of understanding', and the combination, which is always necessary in Christian life, of the *lex orandi* and the *lex credendi*. For example, the catechisms used in Zaire teach in quite an orthodox way that 'God is one God, but there are three persons in him'. Although this formula is recited with fervour, it remains incomprehensible to many people, as one can see during questions in preparing neophytes for baptism, if one moves out of the traditional form of memorized question and answer.

For example, for some people the concept of *persona* sometimes has the connotations of grace (which are themselves vague) and sometimes those of the 'mask' – if the priest, thinking thus to help his hearers to understand the dogma, has committed the pastoral blunder of digressing into Greek thought. For others the whole statement is dissolved in a divine mixture, the ambiguous composition of which is accepted without much understanding. The disappointed understanding thinks it can console itself by evoking the notion of mystery, which is translated *Diswekamu* in Kikongo, *Mobombasmo* in Ligala and *Fumbo* in Swahili. Now these terms derive from the verbal roots *kusweka*, *komoba* and *kufumba*, which mean 'put out of sight of', as one puts money out of the sight of a thief, or 'keep secret', as one keeps secret the 'mysteries' of initiation.

How can one explain in this context that God hides himself and at the same time shows himself in Jesus Christ if the very notion of the revelation of God in Jesus Christ is obscured by the abstruseness generated by the notion of mystery? That God unveils himself as one who is veiled, beyond human grasp and any form of domestication, and that conversely he veils himself as God unveiled, excluding all idols, is a biblical constant. But it is manifestly not what is at issue here, since far from ending up in a negative theology, the process drifts along and becomes an indeterminate fideism which is all too open to the irrational infiltrations of the mystery religions.

Who among the priests working in the African churches has not encountered or at least understood this reproach: 'You Catholic priests have hidden much from us.' In fact it is not the priests who have deliberately hidden anything, but their language which has served to conceal things when faith and the mysteries of salvation are not conveyed in a language or a 'grammar of enunciation' which truly states them. To define inculturation as the process of developing a 'grammar of enunciation' is to give it the task of instituting (or introducing) new languages which express faith in Jesus Christ with the semantics and the syntax of African languages. 'That I may know you and that I may know myself . . .'

(b) A theology of appropriation

Do we have to go on repeating *ad nauseam* formulae which most of the time are never understood and lead to other doubtful ones? People often reply, 'Here we are at the heart of our faith and the trinitarian mystery itself. Consequently, we cannot abandon these dogmas and still be Christians, or at least remain orthodox Catholics.' But who is talking about abandoning dogmas? Certainly one must not separate the envelope from the content too much, since one is the form and the other the substance of the indivisible mystery of Christ, one giving external unity and the other giving unity of substance. But the objection becomes irrelevant and opens up another pespective if one relocates the identity and intelligibility of these dogmas in a logic of the actualization of faith and in the context of the heresies which conditioned their rise and their formulation. Dogma never signifies immutability, but the coaptation of faith in historical structures.

Moreover, without losing any of one's veneration for the fathers and doctors of the church and for all the immemorial stages of Christianity, the African theology of inculturation has to develop a technical vocabulary capable of making strictly intelligible the way in which Africans relate to God and the whole history of redemption while respecting in particular the analogical openness which makes it applicable to divine things. The concept of appropriation expresses this conscious effort by which the theologian and every Christian welcome the word of God and the tradition of the church in their particular existential situation and then try to express it in a way which is distinctive, but reveals the plan of God in their Christian community.

(c) Inculturation as a homeomorphic practice

If the dialogue which inculturation starts up with tradition and other forms of Christian life is not to get caught up in quarrels over history or vocabulary, its approach must be homeomorphic.[23] In the context of the encounter of cultures which are not linked historically, this consists in understanding the otherness which investigating in depth one's own identity and that of the other until common ground or a similar set of problems appear which allow dialogue and the reception of this otherness in one's own categories.

It is this twofold plumbing of one's own depths and the depths of the other, and the topological transformation which that implies, which distinguish homeomorphy from analogy and imitation. Homeomorphy calls for another level of understanding which has to combine the logic of analogical language and that of the functionality of existence. The new words of faith and the grammar of the enunciation of the divine which organizes them into discourse no longer represent more or less approximate translations of other traditions but functional and particular equivalents which are discovered and forged by way of appropriation.

It seems to me that this is the course which John Paul II proposed to the Africans when he declared at Nairobi[24] that inculturation should neither destroy the word of God nor empty the cross of its power (I Cor. 1.17), but that it should introduce Christ to the very heart of African life and raise all African life towards Christ. Christ will only become African in the members of his body when the Africans and African cultures, transformed by the twofold work of the contemplation of Christ and the existential appropriation of faith, produce from their own traditions original expressions of Christian life, celebration and thought.

Translated by John Bowden

Notes

1. Cf. F. Clark, 'Making the Gospel at Home in Asian Cultures', in *Teaching all Nations* (now *East Asian Pastoral Review*) 13, 1976, 131–49; J. -Y. Calvez, 'The Real Problem of Inculturation', *Lumen Vitae* XL, 1985, 70–80.

2. H. de Lubac, *La foi chrétienne. Essai sur la structure du Symbole des Apôtres*, Paris 1969, 255–83.

3. H. Carrier, *Evangile et cultures. De Léon XIII à Jean-Paul II*, Vatican 1987, 202; A. R. Crollius, 'What is so New about Inculturation?', *Gregorianum* 59, 1978, 721–39.

4. M. Amaladoss, 'Dialogue and Mission: Conflict or Convergence?', in *East African Pastoral Review* 1, 1986, 57; A. Pieris, 'Inculturation in Non-Semitic Asia', *The Month* 3, 1986, 86; Eboussi Boulaga, *Christianisme sans fétiche. Révélation et Domination*, Paris 1981, 211.

5. For more details cf. Boka di Mpasi, 'Un jalon sur la voie de l'inculturation', *Revue Africaine de Théologie* 5.10, 1981, 244f.; John Paul II, Speech to Kenyan Bishops, *Documentation catholique* 1787, 1980, 534; id., *Slavorum Apostoli*, Documentation catholique 1900, 1985, 717–24.

6. H. Maurier, 'Situation de l'Eglise catholique au Zaire', *Lumen vitae* 2, 1973, 235–64.

7. See the work from the 1971 theological week at Kinshasa, 'La pertinence du Christianisme en Afrique', *Revue du Clergé Africain* 27, 1972.

8. E. J. Penoukou, *Eglise d'Afrique. Propositions d'avenir*, Paris 1984, 48.

9. Cf. F. Eboussi Boulaga, 'The African Christian in Search of Identity', *Concilium* 106, 1977, 26–34.

10. A. T. Sanon, 'Jesus. Maître d'Initiation', in *Chemins de la Christologie africaine*, Collection Jésus et Jésus-Christ, Paris 1966, p. 144.

11. A. T. Sanon and R. Luneau, *Enraciner l'Evangile. Initiation africaine et Pédagogie de la foi*, Paris, 213.

12. Cf. G. Balandier, *La sociologie actuelle de l'Afrique*, Paris 1982; M. Le Pape and C. Vidal, 'Raisons pratiques africaines', *Cahiers internationaux de Sociologie* LXXII, 1982, 293–321.

13. Eboussi Boulaga, *Christianisme sans fétiche*, 59.

14. F. Eboussi Boulaga, 'Christianisme comme Maladie et comme Guérison', in *Croyance et Guérison*, Collection Etudes et documents africains, Yaoundé 1973, 131.

15. Boulaga, *Christianisme sans fétiche*, 140.

16. M. Hebga, *Emancipation d'Eglises sous tutelle*, Paris 1976, 160.

17. Ibid.

18. Cf. X, 'La théologie africaine. Discours de l'Episcopat zaïrois et de Jean-Paul II', *Revue Africaine de Theologie* 7.14, 1983, 263–71.

19. Paul VI, *Membris Commissionis Theologicae Internationalis, primum plenarium Coetum habentibus*, Acta Apostolicae Sedis LXI, 1969, 713ff.

20. John Paul II, 'Discours aux Evêques des Provinces ecclésiastiques de Kananga et de Lubumbashi', *Revue Africaine de Théologie* 7.14, 1983, 217.

21. Ibid., 271.

22. J. Daniélou, 'Christianisme et Religions non-chrétiennes', *Etudes* 321, 1964; K. Rahner, 'L'avenir de la théologie', *Nouvelle revue théologique* 1, 1971, 12.

23. Cf. R. Panikkar, *Myth, Faith and Hermeneutics*, Maryknoll 1979, 8.

24. John Paul II, *Discours en Afrique*, Rome 1980, 178.

Conclusion: A Historic Occasion or Bureaucratization?

Giuseppe Alberigo

Historical acceleration

The African continent is at a turning point in its history. Following the end of the confrontation between the Atlantic bloc and the Soviet bloc and the inexorable decline of political Marxism, the social and political balance which seemed to have been achieved after the end of the colonial age is showing just how fragile it is. On the one hand the 'balancing' function which the influence of the two imperialisms provided in many areas of the continent has diminished, and on the other the ideological associations have ceased in any way to moderate tribal or 'national' traditions. Finally, the fall of the iron curtain – symbolized by the end of the Berlin wall – has led to the eclipse of the policy of aid to the Third World, relieving the consciences of those on the north of our planet of any inhibitions about returning to a thoroughgoing exploitation of the south. The large-scale and accelerated impoverishment of Africa is obvious to all.

However, it would be unacceptable to limit even a summary survey of the African panorama to the information given immediately above. In fact, everywhere the continent is engaged in the vast historical process of taking its destiny into its own hands and becoming aware of the cultural values of the African traditions. The symbolic value of *Apartheid* makes the ending of it in South Africa, despite all the ambiguities and difficulties associated with it, a potent contribution to this process. It is true that African societies seem particularly defenceless in the face of the aggressive persuasion exercised by the myth of prosperity and consumerism. The impressive exodus of manual workers (often with skills) towards the countries of the North is just one somewhat alarming indication of the growing gap between the poverty of the vast majority and the opulence of very limited groups.

In this new and perhaps unforeseen phase of arduous and painful contradictions, which is also a great catalyst with wide possibilities for the future, the churches and the Christian faith find themselves confronted with a task of epoch-making significance. It is probable that over the next few decades (and perhaps for even longer) the Christian presence in Africa will be shaped by the way in which and to the degree to which this task is fulfilled. In other words, Christians in Africa are at the beginning of a period which will be particularly intense and arduous but also fascinating, a period of testifying to the significance and fertility of the gospel faith. Within a generation the face of the continent will be profoundly changed; there is no human guarantee that it will be inspired by Christianity.

What has been happening recently in various African countries could, however, seem at a hasty glance to be a step in this direction. In fact the collapse of the political leadership sponsored by Soviet imperialism has often meant that the clergy have had to take on social and political responsibilities, to such a degree that an occasional and temporary expedient seems to be turning into a regular and established practice. Conversely, the generally precarious state of public administrative structures is bringing out the stability of the church (and this is perhaps also documented by the growing number of ecclesiastical vocations).

However, it is not unimportant that the church continues to have economic resources, despite the general scarcity of aid. In the light of what has happened in similar circumstances on other continents in past centuries, it should be stated clearly that in the long term, when the prestige of the church has been based on social and political power, this has been a cause of weakness rather than an effective support for evangelization.

This is the context of the decision of John Paul II to convene a special synod for Africa under the title 'You will be my Witnesses', taken from the Acts of the Apostles. So this is a call and an occasion for the Christians of Africa to renew and bring up-to-date their testimony to their faith in God's Christ, who calls on his disciples to bear witness to him not only 'in Jerusalem and throughout Judaea and Samaria', 'but to the ends of the earth' (Acts 1.8).

Council or synod?

At the beginning of the 1960s, the churches of Africa gave a significant response to the convening of the Second Vatican Council by John XXIII. Although they were caught up in the difficult transition from colonial régimes to independence, African Christians (and above all Catholics) saw the epoch-making significance of the occasion and made relevant and unexpected contributions both to the preparatory work[1] and to the council itself.[2] Moreover, the participation of the African episcopate and African theologians in Vatican II gave them opportunities for meetings and discussion in conditions of brotherly equality with bishops and theologians from the other continents, going beyond the sticky subordination which has now become a thing of the past. It is no exaggeration to acknowledge that some of the most significant and lasting decisions of the council, like those on liturgical reform or the rethinking of mission – to take just two examples – could hardly have had such evangelical inspiration and theological richness without the African contribution.

After many centuries, there was thus a reactivation of living communion between African Christianity and the great universal church, a communion which experienced periods of exceptional fertility in antiquity. That had been made possible by the climate of profound renewal created by John XXIII, who also called on the bishops of Africa to find forms of discussion and continental co-operation, like the Pan-African Conference which co-ordinated African participation in Vatican II. Up to that point such co-operation had been non-existent and even unthinkable. This also resulted in an indirect but undeniable contribution to the growth of a continental awareness, which was later institutionalized in the Organization for African Unity.

Globally, Vatican II as a Christian event also gave African Christianity valuable stimuli towards development and renewal, seeds of the gospel, some of which have already borne fruit and others of which are still waiting to yield their produce. In Africa, too, the reception of Vatican II is only in its infancy: it has experienced naivety and impatience and has come up against stubborn resistance and deafness. In more recent years Africa has seemed to prefer a 'prudent' implementation guided by Rome to an active and creative reception. However, Vatican II, by its very nature as a 'pastoral council', requires an active assimilation, which regards the churches as responsible subjects and not just the recipients of decisions made centrally, which are often remote from real needs and are received passively.[3]

In Africa, many people are aware of this, as is evidenced by movements committed to an inculturation of the gospel at all levels of Christian and church experience, from liturgical experimentation to theological reflection on a rethinking of catechesis and the church ministries themselves. The delays suffered by the church in the transition from the colonial phase have made it necessary to condense into a very short period of time both the transition from a 'missionary' régime to an autonomous régime and the replacement of foreign ecclesiastical personnel with indigenous clergy. The effect of this can now be seen in a lack of balance between the plea for autonomy and the effective use of suitable spiritual and cultural energies in its realization.

In the wake of the renewal and open responsibility characteristic of Vatican II, enlightened spirits, above all at the end of the 1960s, began to propose that the churches of Africa should meet in a continental council. The African council was to be held at a continental level and was intended to accelerate the rethinking of the faith in a deep encounter with the cultural and spiritual traditions and the problems of African society. The need was felt to turn the page on the secular symbiosis between faith and colonialism which, though it had had many fruitful outcomes, had also had negative affects. The reciprocal link between the gospel and European culture seemed so substantial and indissoluble that it was preventing the establishment of reciprocal relations with local cultures.

Perplexities and uncertainties

The proposal for a council has prompted some debate in Africa. This has perhaps been killed off by curial mistrust, but it has also been checked by internal difficulties of communication and comprehension; the different sensibilities of the episcopate and clergy of the French-speaking and English-speaking areas have also been a factor. After these uncertainties, the very announcement by the pope at Epiphany 1989 of a Special Synod of Bishops for Africa aroused interest, but also caused perplexity and uncertainty. The perplexity is to be found above all among those who feel the need for an 'African Council'. In their view the decision to celebrate a synod, i.e. a consultative and not a decision-making assembly, is a disappointment in that it qualitatively kills off the petition from which the idea of the council was born. To respond to the request for a decision-making and representative assembly of African Catholicism by announcing a meeting limited to representatives of the episcopal conferences which only has a consultative function seems to many people to evade and distort the original quest for responsibility which grew out of Vatican II.

But John Paul II's announcement has also caused some uncertainty among those who had remained cold or hostile to the proposal for a council. They could not really grasp what lay behind the decision, and were uncertain, not knowing whether Rome really wants an assembly of African Catholics, even in the reduced form of the 'special synod'. Or perhaps, they wonder, may the announcement of the synod simply be skilful camouflage for the ditching of the council? Certainly in these quarters the very machine set in motion for the preparation of the synod[4] has left almost everyone uninterested.

There is a striking difference between the African participation in the preparations for Vatican II, which while perhaps still élitist, was lively and significant, and the lack of interest with which the preparations for the synod have been followed (or perhaps one should say ignored), despite the fact that the commission charged with this is principally made up of representatives of the various African regional episcopal conferences. In reality, so far the synod has remained a 'Roman' initiative, to the degree that not only have all the preparatory meetings been held in Rome, but a number of people think that at least some of the synod itself could be held there. Above all, enthusiasm has been blunted by the control which has been exercised over preparations by the permanent secretariat of the synod and Roman officials. Once again there is a risk that curial zeal will dispossess the local churches of their responsibility and alienate them from an event which should have been aimed above all at stimulating their involvement.

However, it would be an unforgivable mistake if African Catholics passively left the synod to its fate and if the churches of other continents did not help their African sister churches to avoid a mistake of this kind. *Res nostra agitur* – it is our business. It is important to become aware of what is going on. It is true that an episcopal synod is not a council, that a consultative assembly is not a decision-making authority, that 'Synod for Africa' has an undeniably paternalistic ring, as if the African churches were once again to be kept in tutelage. But it is also true that 'synodicality' is increasingly becoming a mark of the present pontificate and that it has a place in the wake of the open ecclesiological renewal brought about by Vatican II. There is no denying that this is still above all a quantitative[5] rather than a qualitative synodicality, but one would have to be blind not to notice the innovative effect of this praxis, simply as a result of the frequency with which synods are held. One has only to reflect on the individualism and isolation characteristic of almost all Catholic bishops up to 1962 to perceive the profound change that is in process towards what is now an emotional cohesion but may soon also be an effective one.

The innovative potential of synodicality is itself inducing the central structures to seek to control and restrict its dynamics, as already happened during the preparation of Vatican II. However, quite apart from the sticking points – which are also irritating – resulting from the survival of the centralism which prevailed prior to Vatican II, and in spite of the foreseeable physiological tensions between the periphery and the centre, there seems to me to be good reason for supposing that historically there is a likelihood of a further consolidation of synodicality at all levels.[6] In fact the initiatives towards the synod are involving the whole continent. This conviction may fuel the expectation that the Synod for Africa will attract considerable attention and may be the basis for a commitment to its success at the highest possible level.

An African approach to synodicality

The nostalgia for the hoped-for African Council cannot kill off commitment to the success of the synod, even if far more is needed for the synod to be a complete success. From this perspective it is essential to expand the involvement of the churches, from the bishops to the last of the faithful, in the preparation – which will last at least a year – and then in the celebration of the synod. The churches have a fruitful and valuable synodical tradition[7] which is being revitalized so that its treasures may be made available for forming 'an African approach to synodicality', which certainly cannot be the parroting of experiences deriving from other cultures and formed in the context of other historical climates.

The synod will be important above all if it is able to express and nurture the growing sense of responsibility in African Catholicism. Regardless of how satisfactory the specific conclusions of the synod may be, what will really matter in determining the future of Christianity in Africa will be the capacity of the synod to *be* the symbolic and meaningful manifestation of communion as the style and norm of the churches of God which are pilgrims in the lands of Africa.[8] Certainly no European can say how this can be realized; only the African community, driven on by the Spirit and through the Spirit discerning the signs of the times, will come to know. This community has a right, but also owes it to the great universal church, to live out and realize the synod as an 'African Pentecost', to use an image dear to John XXIII.

It is quite probable that many obstacles will bar the way in the guise of prudence (carnal), organizational requirements, economic ties, difficulties over accepting one another's differences. Perhaps not all the aspects of the synod will prove to be perfect or admirable, but it will not have failed to show an image of the African Christ to the faithful of Africa, to all Africans, and finally to all men and women. This image may be dim, but it will be faithful and therefore recognizable. An assembly which is capable only of saying what has already been said by others, which is concerned to appear authoritative and powerful, far from the hopes and fears of the brethren, would remain its own prisoner, an arid and ephemeral bureaucratic achievement.

The most optimistic possibility for the synod is that it could become a valauble and significant occasion for embarking on a stage of fuller and wider communion between the African churches. It is important to grasp this possibility of spreading brotherhood, emphasizing both the great shared riches and the specific identities as undeniable components of the African heritage rather than as competing peculiarities. If they are not to waste this opportunity, our African brothers should see this synod as a gift which, through the loving concern of the church of Rome and its bishop, is given by the Spirit to all the churches of Africa, and is not the result of an external initiative against the will of Africans. It is no delusion to wager on the power of the Spirit, above all if such confidence is combined with the unarmed discernment of the sons of light.

It may be that the intention behind the Roman initiative towards the synod has been to avoid an African Council on the grounds that – leaving aside the opposition of some of the episcopate – the pressures towards autonomy to which it could give rise might prove too dangerous. Nor can one fail to note that so far the preparations have marginalized those who are primarily and directly concerned – the Africans. The text of the *Lineamenta* is disconcertingly general, leaving aside the basic problems for Christianity on the African continent. It seems strange that – to give just one example – there is no reference to the complex of problems arising out of the growing impoverishment of the continent, which cannot fail to have a profound effect on the inculturation of the gospel.

The sense questionnaire included as an appendix to the *Lineamenta* is addressed to the bishops (the very approach which had been avoided at the beginning of the preparations for Vatican II). It is purely descriptive, and will almost inevitably result in the collection of superficial responses, unless the African episcopate proves to have a streak of pride or creativity.

And yet it is possible to make the Synod for Africa an evocative occasion, one which would develop the communion which is implicit in and fundamental to the convening of the synod by John Paul II. There is an objective dimension in the pope's action which can and should be implemented, in the spirit of fidelity to the charism of the bishop of Rome.

Does African Catholicism have within itself sufficient energy to follow this trend? The question is being asked in a way which is far from any suspicion of paternalism. But the answer can only be given by African Christians over the next few years, i.e. in the last phase of the preparations for the synod, during the celebration of it, and afterwards, in the years of its reception. Perhaps the synod is an appropriate occasion for a reminder of all the riches of African Christianity, beginning with the glorious traditions which go back to Cyprian and Augustine. We can see that the criterion for the degree of maturity of the pilgrim people of God in Africa is not the recognition that they may be given by the central organs of the church or even by their sister churches from other continents. The sole criterion is how far this people has been faithful to the impulses of the Spirit recognized in the signs of the times.

The inculturation of Christianity in Africa could make a qualitative leap ('a spring forward', as Pope John would have said) if it succeeds in Africanizing the synod from within, exercising a free and serene creativity. The 'fair bride' (Rev. 21.2) will in this way be enriched with new and hitherto unknown precious stones, which the Spirit will hasten to draw from the inexhaustible treasury of the gospel.

Translated by Mortimer Bear

Notes

1. The '*vota*' of the African bishops have been published in *Acta et Documenta concilio oecumenico Vaticano II apparando. Series I antepraeparatoria*, Rome 1960, Vol. II/5. Cf. also the rich volume *Personalité africain et catholicisme*, Paris 1963, which includes the proceedings of the meeting held in Rome to put in perspective the African expectations stemming from Vatican II.

2. Cf. G. Conus, 'L'Eglise d'Afrique au Concile Vatican II', *Neue Zeitschrift für Missionswissenschaft* 30, 1974, 241–55; 31, 1975, 1–19, 124–43.

3. Cf. H. Legrand, 'Le développement d'Eglises-sujets, à la suite de Vatican II. Fondements théologiques et réflections institutionelles', in *Les églises apres Vatican II. Dynamisme et prospective*, ed. G. Alberigo, Paris 1981, 149–84, and also *La réception de Vatican II*, ed. G. Alberigo and J. -P. Jossua, Paris 1985.

4. A chronological table of the preparations for the synod might be useful:

6 January 1989	Announcement by John Paul II, institution of the ante-preparatory commission
7–8 January 1989	First session of the ante-preparatory commission in Rome.
30 January 1989	First circular on the Special Assembly for Africa
1–3 March	Second session of the ante-preparatory commission in Rome.
21–23 June	Nomination of a special council by the secretariat of the Synod of Bishops (which enlarged the ante-preparatory commission) and the first working session in Rome with five topics assigned to five sub-commissions.
14–16 December	Second session of the special council: preparation of the content of the *Lineamenta*: 1. Evangelization; 2. Inculturation; 3. Dialogue; 4. Justice and Peace (two parts); 5. Mass Media.
24–26 January 1990	Rome: the bishops of Verdzekov (Cameroon) and Monsengwo Pasinya (Zaire) edit the *Lineamenta* with the secretariat of the Synod.
22–29 July	Lome: plenary assembly of SECAM; on 14 June Mgr Schotte officially presents the *Lineamenta, The Church in Africa and Its Mission of Evangelization towards the Year 2000: 'You will be my witnesses' (Acts 1.8)*, with 81 questions.
8–10 November	Yamoussoukro: third session of the special council of the secretariat, ending with a speech by the pope;
15–18 January 1991	Rome: fourth session of the special council of the general secretariat on the composition of the synod.

30 November   Deadline for receiving reactions to the *Lineamenta*
6 January 1993   Opening of the Synod

5. Among the contributions published in Africa or in Europe on the prospects for the Synod for Africa are: *La Théologie africaine d'ici au Synode continental africain*, Les nouvelles rationalités africaines 4, 1989; N. Eloki Musey, 'Lieux d'un concile africain', *Neue Zeitschrift für Missionswissenschaft* 45.2, 1989, 138–40; 'Un sinodo per molte Afriche', *Il Regno/Att* 1989/ 18, 524–34; 'Afrika; Erste Leitgedanken für eine Sondersynode', *Herder Korrespondenz* 44, 1990, 407–9; E. -J. Penoukou, 'Les enjeux du Synode africain', *Etudes* 372/6, 1990, 831–42; G. Caprile, 'Primi passi del Sinodo speciale per l'Africa', *La civiltà Cattolica* 141, 1990, no. 3368, 166–74; *La Pentecôte d'Afrique. Synode pour l'Afrique: 1. L'Evènement – 2. Les Attentes, Dec. 1990–Avril 1991*; 'Synode Africain', *Spiritus* 32, 1991, 121–232, Cahier 123.

6. At present preparations are being made for the synod of European bishops, the synod of Latin American bishops (1991: Santo Domingo) and the ordinary synod.

7. An interesting collection of studies has recently been published, edited by Mgr Teissier, Archbishop of Algeria, *La chiesa nell'Africa del norde. Da Tertulliano, Cipriano e Agostino all'attuale islamico*, Milan 1991. This also contains, most opportunely, information on African synodical praxis in antiquity. There are also useful references in G. Ruggieri, *Eglise et Histoire de l'Eglise en Afrique*, Paris 1988.

8. The individual topics are presented in a way which could be aimed just as easily at Christians in any other part of the universal church. The specific African way of treating the issues is given very little space, as is evident even in the choice of the main subjects.

Contributors

MICHEL DUJARIER was born at Tours, France, in 1932. He was ordained priest in 1957, and in 1961 gained a doctorate in theology. For thirty years he has worked in the archdiocese of Cotonou (Benin), where he has pastoral and teaching responsibilities. At present he teaches patrology in the Major Seminary of Ouidah, Benin, and the Catholic Institute of Abidjan, Ivory Coast. His publications are largely about the catechumenate: *Le parrainage des adultes*, 1962; *Catechumenat*, 1969; *Brève histoire du catéchumenat*, 1980; *L'initiation chrétienne des adultes*, 1982. 1991 sees the publication of the first volume of a study on *L'Eglise-Fraternité*.

ELOCHUKWU E. UZUKWU CSSP was born in 1945. At present he is Lecturer in Liturgy and Theology at the Spiritan International School of Theology, Attakwu, Enugu, Nigeria. He has written *Liturgy, Truly Christian Truly African*, Eldoret 1982, and edited *Religion and African Culture. I. Inculturation – A Nigerian Experience*, Enugu 1988; he has also written a number of articles on Christianity in Nigeria.

FRANCISCO JOÃO SILOTA gained a degree in missiology at the Gregorian Institute in 1983 and then did an accountancy course for a few months in Fribourg, Switzerland. After that, in 1984, he was sent as a missionary to Tanzania. In 1988 he was made auxiliary bishop of the archdiocese of Beira, Mozambique, and in January 1991 residential bishop of the newly created diocese of Chimoio.

HENRI TEISSIER was born in Lyons in July 1929. After degrees in arts (at Rabat) and philosophy (at the Sorbonne), he studied theology at the Catholic Institute in Paris (1949–55). He gained a diploma in Arabic and then specialized in Islamic studies at the Dominican Institute of Oriental Studies and the University of Cairo (1956–58). As a priest in the diocese of Algiers he acquired Algerian nationality and became director of the Centre of Languages and Pastoral Studies. Ordained Bishop of Oran in 1973, he returned to Algiers as Coadjutor Archbishop to Cardinal Duval in 1981. He has been Vice-President of Caritas Internationalis since 1987, President of the Episcopal Conference of North Africa since 1982, and a member of the Council of the Secretariat of the Synod from 1983. He has published a number of articles on Islamic-Christian dialogue and the theology of mission, and two books, *Eglise en Islam*, Paris 1984; *La Mission de l'Eglise*, Paris 1985.

JOHN OLORUNFEMI ONAIYEKAN is Co-adjutor Bishop of Abuja, Nigeria's new federal capital, and Apostolic Administrator of Ilorin. Born in 1944, he trained for the priesthood in Nigeria and Rome and was ordained in 1969. After biblical studies at the Pontifical Biblical Institute and the Urban University, Rome, he taught scripture from 1977–82 at the SS Peter and Paul Seminary, Ibadan, where he was also Rector. Between then and his present appointment he was Bishop of Ilorin. He served on the International Theological Commission from 1980 to 1985 and has been on the International Catholic-Methodist Dialogue Commission since 1981. He is on the council for the preparation of the African Synod, and was elected to the Permanent Council for the Synod of Bishops at the 1990 Synod Assembly.

SIMON SEKOMANE MAIMELA was born in Lyndenburg, South Africa, in 1944. He studied at Lutheran Theological College for his BA, and after serving a Lutheran parish he went to Luther Seminary, where he was awarded his ThM. After gaining his PhD at Harvard, he taught at Harvard Divinity School from 1975–1977 and then for a year at Chicago Theological Seminary. In 1981 he was appointed Senior Lecturer at the University of South Africa, where he subsequently became Professor of Systematic Theology. He is the author of six books and has published numerous articles in theological journals. He is currently Africa Co-ordinator of the Ecumenical Association of Third World Theologians and is co-founder and associate editor of the *Journal of Black Theology in South Africa*.

ANDREA RICCARDI was born in 1950 in Rome, where he teaches the history of Christianity at the university La Sapienza; he is interested in contemporary church history and has written, among other books, *Il potere del papa da Pio XII a Paolo VI*, Rome and Bari 1989, and *Il Vaticano e il Cremlino*, Rome and Bari 1992. He is one of the four mediators in the peace negotiations between the Mozambique government and RENAMO, as president of the Community of S.Egidio.

JUSTIN UKPONG is the Deputy Rector of the Catholic Institute of West Africa, Port Harcourt, where he teaches New Testament and African theology. In addition to several journal articles he is the author of *African Theologies Now: A Profile* (1984); *Sacrifice: African and Biblical* (1987); and is currently preparing a book on New Testament perspectives on inculturation.

RENÉ LUNEAU was born in Nantes, France, in 1932. A Dominican and Doctor of Letters, he is a member of the Sociology of Religions Group at the Centre National de la Recherche Scientifique in Paris and teaches at the Catholic Institute in Paris. A specialist on Africa, he has published, by himself or in collaboration, numerous works on contemporary French-speaking Africa and its religious future. He has also been editor of a number of works about the development of the Catholic church since Vatican II: *Le Retour des certitudes. Évènements et orthodoxie depuis Vatican II*, Paris 1987 (with P. Ladrière); *Le Rêve de Compostelle. Vers la restauration d'une Europe chrétienne?*, Paris 1989; *Les Rendez-vous de Saint Domingue. Enjeux d'un anniversaire 1492–1992*, Paris 1991 (with I. Berten).

ROSE ZÓE-OBIANGA was born in 1943 at Bangui in the Central African Republic. She gained a diploma in religious studies in the Faculty of Protestant Theology at Strasbourg and after her master's degree and doctorate spent a year at Union Theological Seminary, New York. She is a lecturer in the Department of African Languages and Linguistics in the Faculty of Letters and Humane Sciences in the University of Yaoundé. She is a member of the Ecumenical Association of African Theologians, of the Ecumenical Association of Third World Theologians, and of Circle. Her publications include 'Questions des femmes africaines à l'Eglise d'Afrique', *Bulletin de Théologie Africaine* 13–14, 1985, 373–81.

KOINIDIS PARTHENIOS, Parthenios III, whose lay name is Aris Koinidis, the 113th Patriarch of Alexandria, was born in 1919 at Port Said, in an exclusively Greek milieu. After his secondary studies at the Greek Schools in Egypt he studied at the theological school of Halki, Constantinople (1936–9), and after the war at the Anglican seminary of Cuddesdon College, Oxford (1946–8). In 1948 Christophoros II, Patriarch of Alexandria (1876–1967), gave him the rank of Archimandrite and appointed him Chief Secretary to the Patriarchate. In 1957 he was elected Metropolitan of Carthage, the newly instituted metropolis, with his seat at Tripoli in Libya. His activity is focussed on his Christian flock made up above all of Greeks in North Africa (Libya, Algeria, Tunisia and Morocco) and Orthodox Arabs. He has written, in French, many books, articles and reports on youth, education, contemporary theology and Christian dialogue, together with some historical studies, the majority published in Alexandria between 1944 and 1964.

BERNARD AGRE is Bishop of Man, Ivory Coast. He was born in 1926 in Monga, one of a family of twelve, and after studies at the Major Seminary of Ouidah in Benin was ordained in 1953. After working in the country parish of Dabou, he became director of the Minor Seminary of Bingerville, where he had also studied; between 1957 and 1960 he gained his doctorate in Rome with a study of indigenous African religious congregations. He then returned to the Ivory Coast to become, first, priest of an urban parish in Abidjan and then vicar general of the archdiocese and a professor at the Major Seminary. He was consecrated bishop of the new diocese of Man in 1968. Between 1985 and 1988 he was President of the Regional Episcopal Conference of Francophone West Africa and from 1989 to 1991 was a member of the pre-preparatory and preparatory commissions for the African Synod.

RIK DE GENDT is a Jesuit with a degree in pedagogical studies from the Catholic University of Louvain, Belgium. He is a journalist for religion and Africa with the Belgian newspaper *Het Volk* and also works in other media.

ENGELBERT MVENG was born in 1930, and has been a Jesuit since 1951. He studied at the universities of Dakar in Senegal, Namur and Louvain in Belgium, and Lyons and the Sorbonne, France, where he gained his doctorate. He was ordained priest in 1963 and since 1965 has been teaching at the university of Yaoundé, Cameroon. He is at present Secretary General of the Ecumenical Association of African Theologians and has published about twenty titles on history, art, anthropology, spirituality, poetry and theology.

METENA M'NTEBA is a Jesuit from Zaire. He teaches at the St Peter Canisius Institute of Philosophy in Kinshasa, but is at present living in Munich, where he is preparing a thesis on political philosophy, after gaining a degree in dogmatic theology at the Gregorian University on the theology of inter-religious dialogue in the recent *magisterium* (1964–1984).

GUISEPPE ALBERIGO was born in 1926 in Varese, and since 1976 has been Professor of Church History in the Faculty of Political Sciences of the University of Bologna. He is also Secretary of the Institute for Religious Sciences of Bologna. His publications include: *I vescovi italiani al concilio di Trento*, 1959; *Lo sviluppo della dottrina sui poteri nella chiesa universale*, 1964; *Cardinalato e collegialità*, 1969; *Chiesa conciliare*, 1981; *Giovanni XXIII. Profezia nella fedeltà*, 1978; *La Chiesa nella Storia*, 1989, and *Nostalgie di unità*, 1989. He has also written and edited a number of studies on Vatican II and has contributed to many historical and theological journals. He is editor of the journal *Cristianesimo nella Storia* and a member of the Board of Directors of *Concilium*.

Editorial Board

Founders

A. van den Boogaard	Nijmegen	The Netherlands
P. Brand	Ankeveen	The Netherlands
Y. Congar OP	Paris	France
H. Küng	Tübingen	Germany
K. Rahner SJ	Innsbruck	Austria
E. Schillebeeckx OP	Nijmegen	The Netherlands

Directors/Counsellors

Giuseppe Alberigo	Bologna	Italy
Willem Beuken SJ	Louvain	The Netherlands
Leonardo Boff	Petrópolis	Brazil
Julia Ching	Toronto	Canada
John Coleman SJ	Berkeley, CA	USA
Christian Duquoc OP	Lyons	France
Virgil Elizondo	San Antonio, TX	USA
Sean Freyne	Dublin	Ireland
Claude Geffré OP	Paris	France
Norbert Greinacher	Tübingen	Germany
Gustavo Gutiérrez	Lima	Peru
Hermann Häring	Nijmegen	The Netherlands
Bas van Iersel SMM	Nijmegen	The Netherlands
Werner Jeanrond	Dublin	Ireland
Jean-Pierre Jossua OP	Paris	France
Nicholas Lash	Cambridge	Great Britain
Kabasele Lunbala	Mbuji Mayi	Zaïre
Mary-John Mananzan OSB	Manila	Philippines
Norbert Mette	Münster	Germany
Johann-Baptist Metz	Münster	Germany
Dietmar Mieth	Neustetten	Germany
Jürgen Moltmann	Tübingen	Germany
Alphonse Ngindu Mushete	Kasai Oriental	Zaïre
Aloysius Pieris SJ	Gonawala-Kelaniya	Sri Lanka
David Power OMI	Washington, DC	USA
James Provost	Washington, DC	USA
Giuseppe Ruggieri	Catania	Italy
Paul Schotsmans	Louvain	Belgium
Lisa Sowle Cahill	Chestnut Hill, MA	USA
Miklós Tomka	Budapest	Hungary
David Tracy	Chicago, IL	USA
Marciano Vidal	Madrid	Spain
Knut Walf	Nijmegen	The Netherlands
Anton Weiler	Heelsum	The Netherlands
Christos Yannaras	Athens	Greece

General Secretariat: Prins Bernhardstraat 2, 6521 AB Nijmegen, The Netherlands
Secretary: Mrs E. C. Duindam-Deckers

Other Issues of *Concilium* to be published in 1992

The New Europe - A Challenge for Christians
edited by N.Greinacher and N.Mette

1992 sees a major step in the development of the European community. This issue considers the changes that it will bring and others which are needed; the political and ethical challenges posed to Europe by the rest of the world; and the special role of the churches in the new Europe.

1992/2   April

Fundamentalism in the World's Religions
edited by Hans Küng and Jürgen Moltmann

Begins by defining fundamentalism from both a theological and sociological perspective; looks at the challenge of contemporary Jewish and Muslim and Christian (Orthodox, Catholic and Protestant) fundamentalism and possible answers to it; discusses the relationship of fundamentalism to both modernity and postmodernity.

1992/3   June

God, Where are You? A Cry in the Night
edited by Christian Duquoc and Casiano Florestan

Studies especially the silence of God in the modern world. It examines the absence of God in the Bible; in the experience of Jewish poets; in sickness; in the suffering of women, the exploited and the humiliated; in distress arising from sin and in death; and looks at the significance of this silence for church institutions.

1992/4   August

The Taboo on Democracy in the Church
edited by James Provost and Knut Walf

It is widely held that democracy is incompatible with the nature of the Catholic Church. This issue questions that assumption by examining both democracy and the nature of the church. It considers the ecclesiological implications of the theme; gives examples of democratic structures; and makes concrete proposals for the future.

1992/5   October

The Debate on Modernity
edited by Claude Geffre and Jean-Pierre Jossua

It is widely said that the modern world is now a thing of the past; we have now moved on to post-modernity. This issue looks at definitions of modernity and its relationship to Christianity; at the rise of post-modernity and criticisms of it; and at possible Christian strategies in the face of the crisis for modernity.

1992/6   December

DATE DUE

MY 21 '74	NOV 20 1998		
E 16 '75		DISCARDED	
MY 28 '75			
OC 29 '75			
MY _ 7 '84			
OCT 8 '93			
MAY 3 '94			
GAYLORD			PRINTED IN U.S.A.

DATE DUE

DISCARDED